Kia J. Bentley, PhD, LCSW
Editor

Psychiatric Medication Issues for Social Workers, Counselors, and Psychologists

Psychiatric Medication Issues for Social Workers, Counselors, and Psychologists has been co-published simultaneously as *Social Work in Mental Health,* Volume 1, Number 4 2003.

Pre-publication REVIEWS, COMMENTARIES, EVALUATIONS . . .

"WILL LIKELY APPEAL TO A WIDE RANGE OF PRO-FESSIONALS–social workers, psychologists, and counselors of all sorts. . . . Provides a critical perspective of psychiatric medication in clinical practice. The book is designed to facilitate better service to adults and children. It casts a wide net and the catch includes a rapid assessment tool for ascertaining the impact of medication on a client, the emerging 'illness identity' similar to the 'sick role,' medication management, and the role of complementary practice as a supplement to conventional treatment."

Kevin Corcoran, PhD, JD
Professor
School of Social Work
Portland State University

Psychiatric Medication Issues for Social Workers, Counselors, and Psychologists

Psychiatric Medication Issues for Social Workers, Counselors, and Psychologists has been co-published simultaneously as *Social Work in Mental Health,* Volume 1, Number 4 2003.

Social Work in Mental Health Monographic "Separates"

Below is a list of "separates," which in serials librarianship means a special issue simultaneously published as a special journal issue or double-issue _and_ as a "separate" hardbound monograph. (This is a format which we also call a "DocuSerial.")

"Separates" are published because specialized libraries or professionals may wish to purchase a specific thematic issue by itself in a format which can be separately cataloged and shelved, as opposed to purchasing the journal on an on-going basis. Faculty members may also more easily consider a "separate" for classroom adoption.

"Separates" are carefully classified separately with the major book jobbers so that the journal tie-in can be noted on new book order slips to avoid duplicate purchasing.

You may wish to visit Haworth's website at . . .

http://www.HaworthPress.com

. . . to search our online catalog for complete tables of contents of these separates and related publications.

You may also call 1-800-HAWORTH (outside US/Canada: 607-722-5857), or Fax 1-800-895-0582 (outside US/Canada: 607-771-0012), or e-mail at:

docdelivery@haworthpress.com

Psychiatric Medication Issues for Social Workers, Counselors, and Psychologists, edited by Kia J. Bentley, PhD, LCSW (Vol. 1, No. 4, 2003). _OUTSTANDING. . . . All social workers, counselors, and psychologists working in the mental health field would benefit from reading this outstanding book. (Deborah P. Valentine, PhD, MSSW, Professor and Director, School of Social Work, Colorado State University)_

Psychiatric Medication Issues
for Social Workers, Counselors, and Psychologists

Kia J. Bentley, PhD, LCSW
Editor

Psychiatric Medication Issues for Social Workers, Counselors, and Psychologists has been co-published simultaneously as *Social Work in Mental Health,* Volume 1, Number 4 2003.

The Haworth Social Work Practice Press
An Imprint of The Haworth Press, Inc.

New York • London • Victoria (AU)
www.HaworthPress.com

Published by
The Haworth Social Work Practice Press®, 10 Alice Street, Binghamton, NY 13904-1580 USA
The Haworth Social Work Practice Press® is an imprint of The Haworth Press, Inc., 10 Alice
Street, Binghamton, NY 13904-1580 USA.

Psychiatric Medication Issues for Social Workers, Counselors, and Psychologists has been co-published simultaneously as *Social Work in Mental Health,*™ Volume 1, Number 4 2003.

The development, preparation, and publication of this work has been undertaken with great care. However, the publisher, employees, editors, and agents of The Haworth Press and all imprints of The Haworth Press, Inc., including The Haworth Medical Press® and Pharmaceutical Products Press®, are not responsible for any errors contained herein or for consequences that may ensue from use of materials or information contained in this work. Opinions expressed by the author(s) are not necessarily those of The Haworth Press, Inc. With regard to case studies, identifies and circumstances of individuals discussed herein have been changed to protect confidentiality. Any resemblance to actual persons, living or dead, is entirely coincidental.

Cover design by Lora L. Wiggins

Library of Congress Cataloging-in-Publication Data

Psychiatric medication issues for social workers, counselors, and psychologists / Kia J. Bentley, editor.
      p. cm.
    "Co-published simultaneously as Social work in mental health, vol. 1, no. 4, 2003."
    Includes bibliographical references and index.
    ISBN 0-7890-2400-4 (hard cover : alk. paper)–ISBN 0-7890-2401-2 (soft cover : alk. paper)
    1. Medical social work. I. Bentley, Kia J. II. Social work in mental health.
HV687P78 2003
362.2–dc22   2003022887

Indexing, Abstracting & Website/Internet Coverage

This section provides you with a list of major indexing & abstracting services. That is to say, each service began covering this periodical during the year noted in the right column. Most Websites which are listed below have indicated that they will either post, disseminate, compile, archive, cite or alert their own Website users with research-based content from this work. (This list is as current as the copyright date of this publication.)

(continued)

Special Bibliographic Notes related to special journal issues
(separates) and indexing/abstracting:

- indexing/abstracting services in this list will also cover material in any "separate" that is co-published simultaneously with Haworth's special thematic journal issue or DocuSerial. Indexing/abstracting usually covers material at the article/chapter level.
- monographic co-editions are intended for either non-subscribers or libraries which intend to purchase a second copy for their circulating collections.
- monographic co-editions are reported to all jobbers/wholesalers/approval plans. The source journal is listed as the "series" to assist the prevention of duplicate purchasing in the same manner utilized for books-in-series.
- to facilitate user/access services all indexing/abstracting services are encouraged to utilize the co-indexing entry note indicated at the bottom of the first page of each article/chapter/contribution.
- this is intended to assist a library user of any reference tool (whether print, electronic, online, or CD-ROM) to locate the monographic version if the library has purchased this version but not a subscription to the source journal.
- individual articles/chapters in any Haworth publication are also available through the Haworth Document Delivery Service (HDDS).

ABOUT THE EDITOR

Kia J. Bentley, PhD, LCSW, is Professor and Director of the PhD Program in Social Work at Virginia Commonwealth University where she has taught since 1989. Dr. Bentley has a BSW from Auburn University, an MSSW from the University of Tennessee and a PhD from Florida State, where she received a "Distinguished Alumna Award" in 1997. She is the author of the 2001 book, now in its second edition, *The Social Worker & Psychotropic Medication* (with Joseph Walsh, Brooks/Cole) and is the editor of the 2002 text *Social Work Practice in Mental Health: Contemporary Roles, Tasks & Techniques* (Brooks/Cole). Her journal publications discuss the social worker's role in medication management, the right to refuse medication, family psychoeducation, peer leadership training for consumers, prescription writing privileges for social workers, and women and mental health. She is the coordinator of this conference as part of her role as Principal Investigator on the project called "Best practices for clinical social workers in psychopharmacotherapy," funded by the Ittleson Foundation in NYC. She is also a member of a national Internet panel that focuses on "Psychopharmacology for Psychotherapists," sponsored by PsyBroadcasting. She currently serves as Chair of Central State Hospital's Human Rights Committee, a state psychiatric facility in Petersburg, Virginia.

Psychiatric Medication Issues for Social Workers, Counselors, and Psychologists

CONTENTS

About the Contributors

Sarah Bradley, LCSW, is an instructor at Portland State University School of Social Work, where she teaches foundation and advanced classes in practice methods. She has also taught social work courses for the University of Washington and Virginia Commonwealth University, as well as postgraduate courses for the Certificate Program in Clinical Theory and Practice in Seattle. She is an MSSW graduate of Columbia University School of Social Work and the New York School for Psychoanalytic Psychotherapy, and is a past Board Member of the Washington State Society for Clinical Social Work. She has over twenty years of clinical and supervisory experience with clients with mental health issues and has published and lectured on aspects of integrating psychotherapy and psychopharmacology into clinical practice among nonphysicians. She serves as the moderator of an on-going series, "Psychopharmacology for Psychotherapists," for PsyBroadcasting, an Internet provider of continuing education and the technical manager of this conference.

David Cohen, PhD, is Professor of Social Work and Director of the PhD program in social welfare at Florida International University, Miami. He received his BA from McGill University, his MSW from Carleton University, and his PhD in Social Welfare from the University of California at Berkeley. He has co-authored or edited 8 books and 60 publications, mostly on clinical, iatrogenic, and withdrawal effects of psychotropic drugs, their sociocultural uses, and methods used to evaluate their safety and efficacy. These include the book *Your Drug May Be Your Problem: How and Why to Stop Taking Psychiatric Medications* (1999, Perseus) which is reviewed at this conference, and *Tardive Dyskinesia and Cognitive Dysfunction* (1993), *Challenging the Therapeutic State* (1990), and in French, *Medicalization and Social Control* (1994), and *Critical Handbook of Psychiatric Drugs* (1995). He is Editor of *Ethical Human Sciences and Services*, an international journal of critical inquiry, and is an editorial board member of four journals in psychology and social work. He has presented his research findings in departments of psychiatry, in hospital grand rounds, in schools of law, before state legislatures, and as a consultant in legal proceedings. Dr. Cohen is President of the non-profit International Center for the Study of Psychiatry and Psychology, based in New York, and he maintains a part-time counseling practice.

Sophia F. Dziegielewski, PhD, is Professor in the School of Social Work, University of Central Florida, Orlando, having taught previously at the University of Alabama and Meharry Medical College in Nashville. She earned both her MSW and PhD degrees in Social Work from Florida State University. Her vita boasts over 70 publications and five books in the area of health and mental health including *Social Work Practice and Psychopharmacology* (2001, Springer Series on Social Work), *DSM-IV-TR in Action* (2002, Springer), and *The Changing Face of Health Care* (1998, Springer). Among numerous academic and professional honors, she was given University Award for Excellence in Graduate Teaching and also the University Faculty Leadership Award (2002) at the University of Central Florida, and Tennessee chapter of National Association of Social Workers (NASW) Social Worker of the Year in 1995. Her professional interests primarily focus on health and mental health issues, time-limited evidenced-based practice strategies, and the establishment of outcome-based interventions. Active in clinical practice throughout her career, she gives frequent workshops and community presentations on different types of mental health related counseling practices and sftategies in today's managed care environment.

Rosemary L. Farmer, PhD, LCSW, is Associate Professor of Social Work at Virginia Commonwealth University (VCU) where she teaches graduate courses in clinical practice, human behavior, and psychopharmacology for social workers. She received her MSW degree from the Hunter College and her PhD from VCU. She has published in such journals as *British Journal of Social Work, Health & Social Work*, and *Journal of Social Work Education*. She has been a clinical social work practitioner for 30 years, specializing in work with persons who have chronic and serious mental illnesses. She also has a long-standing interest in public mental health services and has served as a consultant to staff at the Northern Virginia Mental Health Institute, and as a researcher at a Veterans Administration Mental Hygiene Clinic and community residential programs. She is a founding board member of Gateway Homes in Richmond, an innovative group home for persons with serious mental illness. Her research interests include major mental illnesses and incorporating more biological knowledge into social work theorizing and practice. Currently she is a research associate on the VCU project to develop knowledge around "Best Practices for Clinical Social Workers in Psychopharmacotherapy."

Jerry Floersch, PhD, joined Case Western Reserve University's Mandel School of Applied Social Sciences faculty in 1999. He earned his MSW from the University of Kansas and his PhD from the University of Chicago School of Social Service Administration. Dr. Floersch's articles have appeared in *Culture, Medicine and Psychiatry* and *Psychiatric Rehabilitation Journal*. His first book, called *Meds, Money, and Manners: The Case Management of Severe Mental Illness* (2002), which is reviewed at this conference, was recently published by Columbia University Press. By comparing the oral and written narratives of case managers, the book examines the rise of community support services, the rise of the case manager and case management, and the limits of management models in providing effective services. He has twenty years of direct practice experience with various at-risk populations and ethnic groups, both urban and suburban. He is currently conducting research on medication management and is in the final year of a three-year study funded by the Ohio Department of Mental Health of a new case management model called "Recovery."

Janis Jenkins, PhD, is currently Professor of Anthropology and Psychiatry at Case Western Reserve and a medical anthropologist who specializes in the study of culture and experience, mental illness (schizophrenia, depression, and trauma), gender and development, women's studies, political violence, Latin America, the Caribbean, and U. S. Latinos. She is a UCLA PhD graduate. Dr. Jenkins has recently completed editing a book (with R.J. Barrett) called *The Edge of Experience: Schizophrenia, Culture, and Subjectivity* (2003), Cambridge University Press) and finished a three-year, NIMH funded qualitative study of the subjective experience of adults on antipsychotic medications. The research was launched in an effort to move beyond studies of medication "compliance" and "adherence" to specify empirically the subjective experience and meaning of taking medication from the perspectives of persons taking them.

Jill Littrell, PhD, is Professor in the School of Social Work at Georgia State University where she has taught since 1992. She received an MSSW in 1972 from the University of Wisconsin at Madison and then worked for many years in child welfare, at a state psychiatric hospital, and in residential treatment for adolescent girls. Following this, she returned to school and received a PhD in clinical psychology from Arizona State University in 1982. She worked in the Department of Drug and Alcohol Dependence at CIGNA Health Plan for five years while writing a two-volume work on alcoholism, *Understanding and Treating Alcoholism*

(Lawrence Erlbaum). Dr. Littrell has published extensively on issues related to mental health and substance abuse, including in *Social Work Research*, *Journal of Social Work Research*, *Health & Social Work*, *Journal of Sociology and Social Welfare*, *Community Mental Health Journal*, and *Journal of Social Work Practice with Addictions*. She is currently working on a master's degree in Biology in order to develop a research agenda in the emerging field of psychoneuroimmunology.

Jeffrey Longhofer, PhD, is Adjunct Associate Professor at the Mandel School for Applied Social Sciences & Department of Anthropology at Case Western Reserve University and a clinic associate in the Hanna Perkins Center for Child Development. He earned his PhD in Anthropology from the University of Kansas and has just recently completed his MSW from Smith College. His most recent work focuses on how mental health practice intersects with chronic and terminal illness across the life span and in the nature of individual's transition from physical medical services to mental health services, or vice versa, is accomplished. His work is aimed at understanding the multi-level sites where chronic mental and physical illness intersect to produce biographical disruptions, narrative reconstruction's, renegotiated senses of selfhood and positive action aimed at the production of well-being. In a forthcoming article in the *American Journal of Orthopsychiatry*, he uses qualitative and ethnographic methods to understand medication management in chronic mental illness. He is also interested in medication and identity formation.

Melissa Floyd Taylor, PhD, LCSW, is Assistant Professor of Social Work at the University of North Carolina, Greensboro. She completed her doctoral work at Virginia Commonwealth University (VCU) in 2002 after receiving her MSW from VCU in 1994. She received her undergraduate degrees in psychology and political science from Miami University in Oxford, Ohio. She recently co-authored a debate on outpatient commitment in *Controversial Issues in Social Policy* (2003, Allyn/Bacon) as well as a chapter on excellence in contemporary practice in *Social Work Practice in Mental Health* (2002, Brooks/Cole). Throughout her career, she has worked in direct service settings, primarily with persons who have serious mental illness, substance abuse issues, or both. Her current research interests include the operationailization of social work values in practice with persons who have serious Mental Illness. Specifically, she has investigated the intersection of involuntary interventions in mental health with the social work value of self-determination and the impact of this possible conflict on social workers. She is currently exploring creative, consumer-driven alternatives to involuntary interventions.

Joseph Walsh, PhD, LCSW, is Associate Professor of Social Work at Virginia Commonwealth University (VCU). He has both his MSW and his PhD from the Ohio State University. With colleague Kia J. Bentley, he is co-author of *The Social Worker and Psychotropic Medication*, and is also the author of *Clinical Case Management with Persons Having Mental Illness*, both published by Brooks/Cole, and *Endings in Clinical Practice* (2003), Lyceum Press) as well as dozens of journal publications on related topics. Dr. Walsh has been a direct service practitioner in the field of mental health since 1974, first in a psychiatric hospital, later in community mental health center, and now in a university counseling center. He has been at VCU since 1993, and teaches courses in generalist practice, clinical practice, research, mental and emotional disorders, and social and behavioral science theory. His research interests are in the areas of clinical social work practice, serious mental illness, and psychopharmacology. Currently he is a research associate on the VCU project to develop knowledge around "Best Practices for Clinical Social Workers in Psychopharmacotherapy."

Introduction

Welcome, welcome, welcome to this special volume! Here the reader is exposed to critical perspectives on the use of psychiatric medication in clinical practice, as well as creative ideas on how social workers and other allied health providers can be more responsive to both adults and children who take these kinds of medication. Readers will review interesting qualitative and quantitative research that explores the subjective experience of clients who use psychiatric medication, as well as practitioner dilemmas in helping them to manage and monitor it. Readers will also consider the implications of current research for informed consent and the negotiation of complex collaborative relationships with both clients and prescribing physicians. With an eye toward the future, readers will be invited to consider the safety of herbal preparations and the future role of non-medical providers in medication management. Here is a taste of what the authors specifically offer you in this collection of articles.

Long a critic of psychiatric medication, David Cohen presents his *Psychiatric Medication History: An Interview Schedule* (PMHIS). This 30-question protocol is offered in hopes of helping "practitioners understand how their clients manage their psychotropic medications and interpret their effects." Use of this clinical tool refocuses the social worker's attention toward the meaning of medication to clients, and their positive and negative subjective experiences with them over time. This would be a welcome and much needed philosophical shift away from the current overemphasis on issues related to compliance. Sarah Bradley then reminds us that the centrality of *meanings* regarding psychiatric medication is not limited to clients, but is relevant to social

[Haworth co-indexing entry note]: "Introduction." Bentley, Kia J. Co-published simultaneously in *Social Work in Mental Health* (The Haworth Social Work Practice Press, an imprint of The Haworth Press, Inc.) Vol. 1, No. 4, 2003, pp. 1-3; and: *Psychiatric Medication Issues for Social Workers, Counselors, and Psychologists* (ed: Kia J. Bentley) The Haworth Social Work Practice Press, an imprint of The Haworth Press, Inc., 2003, pp. 1-3. Single or multiple copies of this article are available for a fee from The Haworth Document Delivery Service [1-800-HAWORTH, 9:00 a.m. - 5:00 p.m. (EST). E-mail address: docdelivery@haworthpress.com].

http://www.haworthpress.com/web/SWMH
Digital Object Identifier: 10.1300J200v01n04_01

workers (and all providers) as well. We also bring our own personalities, attachment styles, expectations, attitudes and beliefs about medication to the practice "table," and these greatly influence not only our interactions with clients but collaborative processes among providers. Bradley relies on familiar terms "transference" and "countertransference" to frame her discussion. Likewise, Jerry Floersch's concern is about the psychological impact of the "illness identity" of children and adolescents in particular and its relationship to the "growing acceptance of the disease model" and the conceptualization of childhood psychiatric disorders as "illnesses." His arguments point to the powerful and worrisome influence of medical rhetoric in use around psychiatric medication today. Similarly, he and his colleagues Jeffrey Longhofer and Janis Jenkins introduce the notion of drug *aporia*, defined as an "interpretive gap between a client's desired and perceived effects of psychotropic drug treatment." They offer up an interesting model for making sense of all the complex interactions between case management relationships and events related to drug management processes.

Using data from the first-ever national study on social work roles with psychiatric medication, my colleagues Joe Walsh, Rosemary Farmer, Melissa Floyd Taylor, and I present common ethical dilemmas experienced by a large randomly selected group of experienced NASW members. The most common dilemmas, such as respecting a client's right to decline medication, concerns about over or undermedication or long wait lists, and grey areas involving coercion or advocacy, for example, seem to stem from the dual interest in paternalism and self-determination, and the challenging sometimes frustrating interactions with psychiatrists or external forces such as managed care. Jill Littrell builds on the cross-cutting theme of ethics. As a PhD psychologist on a social work faculty, she is in an interesting position to challenge the social worker's role in providing informed consent to clients considering the use of psychiatric medication. She affirms the "imperative" of social workers to discuss medication with clients experiencing mental health related difficulties, but "how much and what kind of information" seems to be the crucial question of her paper, and a central question for us as social work practitioners and educators.

Finally, Sophia Dziegielewski calls on social workers to expand their knowledge about "complementary" practices. After summarizing a number of alternative medicine approaches that are used by clients, she challenges us to consider the problems that result from a lack of full knowledge or the actual misuse of herbal preparations, essential oils, and flower essences. The bottom line is that education about psychopharmacology must include the dimension of herbal medicine, including the empirical foundation of these approaches. The same critical perspective that social workers need to bring to bear on more typical psychiatric medications must be imported to this topic as well.

All the papers are final versions of those that were part of *The First National Internet Conference on Social Work & Psychopharmacology*, which took place over the course of three weeks in February 2003. That conference was part of a larger project funded by the Ittleson Foundation called "Best Practices for Clinical Social Work in Psychopharmacotherapy," which has involved the national survey discussed here and the development of curriculum modules and consultation site visits to Schools of Social Work (reported on elsewhere). I served as PI on that project with my colleagues Joe and Rosemary serving as research associates. The Internet conference itself consisted of shared on-line moderated discussions of these invitational papers. Participants read the papers which had been uploaded onto the electronic library of Psy Broadcasting Company (PsyBC.com), a Web-based continuing education provider. They then visited bulletin boards to post comments, or just "listened" to what others had to say. That conference *and* this special volume share a simple mission: to serve as an innovative forum and an effective springboard for productive discussion among practitioners, scholars, and researchers about psychiatric medication's relevance to, and interface with, social work practice. The hope then is that this provocative collection of articles will reinvigorate the conversation about social work's contemporary role in mental health practice in the midst of an era of biological psychiatry. It goes out with tremendous heartfelt gratitude to the contributing authors for the courage, wisdom, and commitment they each bring to bear in this scholarly arena.

Kia J. Bentley, PhD, LCSW
Virginia Commonwealth University

The Psychiatric Medication History:
Context, Purpose, and Method

David Cohen

SUMMARY. This article presents *The Psychiatric Medication History: An Interview Schedule*, a 30-step semi-structured protocol designed to help practitioners understand how clients manage their psychotropic medications and interpret their effects. The critical perspective leading to the design of this interview schedule, its purposes for clients and practitioners, its divergence from traditional treatment histories, and its uses and limitations are discussed. The author contends that, in a safe space, taking a psychiatric medication history according to these suggested guidelines offers clients an opportunity to construct an independent, evidence-tested personal narrative about their medication use. To practitioners, taking such a medication history offers a person-in-environment point of entry into the psychopharmacology scene. *[Article copies available for a fee from The Haworth Document Delivery Service: 1-800-HAWORTH. E-mail address: <docdelivery@haworthpress.com> Website: <http://www.HaworthPress.com> © 2003 by The Haworth Press, Inc. All rights reserved.]*

KEYWORDS. Psychopharmacology, social work, medication history

The original version of this paper was initially presented at the First National Internet Conference on Social Work & Psychopharmacology, February 3-24, 2003, sponsored by the Ittleson Foundation and the Virginia Commonwealth University School of Social Work in association with Psy Broadcasting Company.

[Haworth co-indexing entry note]: "The Psychiatric Medication History: Context, Purpose, and Method." Cohen, David. Co-published simultaneously in *Social Work in Mental Health* (The Haworth Social Work Practice Press, an imprint of The Haworth Press, Inc.) Vol. 1, No. 4, 2003, pp. 5-28; and: *Psychiatric Medication Issues for Social Workers, Counselors, and Psychologists* (ed: Kia J. Bentley) The Haworth Social Work Practice Press, an imprint of The Haworth Press, Inc., 2003, pp. 5-28. Single or multiple copies of this article are available for a fee from The Haworth Document Delivery Service [1-800-HAWORTH, 9:00 a.m. - 5:00 p.m. (EST). E-mail address: docdelivery@haworthpress.com].

Within the mental health system, the place of medication is pivotal and in everyday discourse the word "treatment" is synonymous with "medication." In the West, for the past half-century, there has been systematic use of about one hundred psychotropic drugs. Hundreds of millions of people have been prescribed these drugs for dozens of emotional/behavioral states. Thousands of scientists have investigated the drugs' effectiveness. As a result, colossal revenues have been generated for drug manufacturers. Still, no current data shows even modest improvements in the incidence or prevalence or prognosis of *any* condition routinely treated today with psychotropics, including schizophrenia, bipolar disorder, and depression (Cohen, 1997a; Healy, 1997; Research Triangle Institute, 2002; Whitaker, 2002). Nonetheless, prescribing psychotropics to more people, to younger people, and for longer periods, is continually increasing (e.g., Zito et al., 2003), and expansions of coercive psychiatric interventions (such as outpatient commitment) appear intertwined with the popularity of drugs.

Two decades ago, practicing social workers merely referred patients for medication. Today, social workers may be involved in many more medication-related tasks. These tasks include recommending that physicians prescribe drugs to clients, monitoring medicated clients' states, persuading or coercing clients to follow prescribed drug regimen, facilitating clients' understanding of drug effects, and assisting clients to stop taking drugs. Case managers of clients diagnosed with severe mental illness and residing outside hospitals may count and sort medication boxes, bring drugs to clients' homes and watch while clients take them, and drive clients to and from clinic appointments where medication is the overriding issue of interest (Floersch, 2002). These activities of case managers literally make possible the taking of medications by clients within a service system arguably revolving around "medication compliance."

Few textbooks on social work and psychopharmacology have been published, and courses on this topic are the exception in social work curricula. Most social workers receive only cursory training in this area, which suggests that they are not provided with the opportunity to evaluate their involvement critically. One can speculate that where social workers take part in medication-related activities, training is on-the-job: guided by the requirements and the short-term goals of the service, provided by a multidisciplinary team or medical professional, or using information and guidelines from one's employer. This is not to suggest that practitioners blindly follow dictates to monitor drug treatments without grappling with the significance of these treatments in their clients' lives and in relation to their helping strategies. Indeed, in the only detailed narration of case managers' work on a daily basis in mental health settings, Floersch (2002) reveals subtle processes of managing medications and interpreting their effects. However, Floersch's analysis confirms that such processes become visible and intelligible only if the observer attempts methodically to uncover them. In this effort, he or she must be guided by various conjectures and hypotheses about the observed situation, including a critical understanding of the goals of the treatment system.

In this vein, this article presents *The Psychiatric Medication History: An Interview Schedule* (see Table 1). This schedule was designed to help practitioners obtain information from their clients to help decode their clients' procedures of managing medications and interpreting their effects. The schedule grew out of interviews the author conducted as advocate, medication consultant, researcher, and therapist with adult users of psychiatric drugs. It was further developed in group meetings and workshops with such users. The schedule is part of this author's effort to assist social work practitioners and students to emancipate from the domination of the medical model (the view that people who behave in ways unapproved or unacceptable have something wrong with their genes/brains and that this problem needs to be fixed physically). The schedule may also help to ground some social work interventions on an independently-arrived-at knowledge base, explicitly guided by the intention to minimize iatrogenic harm and redress power imbalances between clients and professionals (Cohen, 1988, 2002; Cohen & Jacobs, 2000). Finally, the schedule fits in the author's broader attempt to formulate a critical, constructivist, and systems framework within social work to conceptualize and study medication use in individuals and societies (Cohen et al., 2001).

The article is structured as follows: in the major portion of the text, some critical conjectures and observations shaping the author's perspective on psychiatric medication are outlined. Next, to provide contrast and additional context, literature bearing on treatment/medication histories in psychiatry is analyzed. Finally, uses and limitations for social work practice of *The Psychiatric Medication History: An Interview Schedule* are discussed.

CRITICAL THINKING ABOUT PSYCHIATRIC DRUGS

A pressing task facing mental health professionals today may be analogized to a "detoxification" process: identifying and examining

TABLE 1. The Psychiatric Medication History: An Interview Schedule

---

Baseline

1. Ask subject to describe his/her most important current difficulties.

2. Ask subject to describe what he/she believes would be the most helpful intervention (resource, person, skill, thing, etc.) for him/her at this time.

3. Ask subject to identify what he/she believes are the main obstacles to getting this help.

   Names and instructions

4. Record names and dosages of all drugs currently taken by the subject, including prescribed medications and licit or illicit drugs.

5. Record any name given to each drug by the subject (e.g., "tranquilizer," "little red pill," etc.)

6. Ask subject to explain why each drug is taken, and for how long each has been taken.

7. Ask subject to describe any instructions received from physician or nurse regarding the taking of the prescribed medications.

8. Ask subject which side or adverse effects, if any, he/she has been told to expect or has discussed with health professional. When did these discussions take place, and how often?

Compliance

9. Inquire about the regularity of drug consumption (continuous, intermittent, idiosyncratic, etc.) and adherence to physician's instructions.

First Use

10. How does subject describe his/her difficulties when prescribed drug use first started? Inquire into the particular circumstances and events immediately preceding drug use.

11. How does subject describe the *initial* effect of drugs on the above difficulties? Inquire if and how the use of drugs modified the circumstances and events.

12. Inquire into subsequent episodes of drug use if the initial drug taking was discontinued.

Effects

13. How does subject describe the current effects of medication on his/her functioning?

14. How does subject think the drugs act upon his/her body or mind?

15. How does subject describe the effects of medication on interaction with other people, general well-being, looking for employment, reading, writing, remembering things, working and being attentive, interacting with his or her family?

16. How does subject describe the effects of medication on sleeping and waking, sexual desire, lovemaking, urinating and having bowel movements, sweating, sensitivity to light?

17. Ask subject to name the distinctive "psychological" effect or effects of their medication. If subject had to give his/her own descriptive label to the medication, what would it be?

18. Ask subject to name the distinctive "physical" effect or effects of their medication.

19. Ask subject whether drugs consistently have the same effect on him/her.

TABLE 1 (continued)

Non-drug solutions

20. Ask subject if and how current difficulties are similar to difficulties leading to original drug use.

21. Ask subjects if other solutions besides drug use were attempted, and if so, with whom and with what results? Ask subject whether/what lessons were gained from these attempts.

Withdrawal

22. Ask subject to describe any attempts made to reduce dosage or completely cease taking medication. Inquire into why subject acted and whether these attempts were discussed with others.

23. Ask subject to describe as precisely as possible the withdrawal schedule used.

24. Ask subject to describe what occurred during and after withdrawal.

25. Inquire about the negative and positive effects of the withdrawal experience.

26. Ask subject if and how much of the withdrawal experience was discussed with health professionals. Ask subject whether/what lessons were gained from these discussions.

Social network

27. Ask subject to describe the attitudes of family members about his/her medication use.

28. Ask subject to describe the attitudes of health professionals about his/her medication use.

29. Ask subject to describe the last three different conversations he/she had with anyone about his/her medication use.

Conclusion

30. Ask subject what he/she wishes to understand better about his/her medication use.

some deeply held or "simply held" ideas and deciding whether or not one should continue to hold them (Cohen, 2001). The reason to do so is that most ideas (hypotheses, theories) and their associated interventions (technologies, practices) representing reform, progress or enlightenment at one moment in the history of mental health interventions were later repudiated as misleading or damaging (e.g., Braslow, 1997; Johnson, 1990). Proponents of these ideas were leaders and practitioners of the mental health professions and their allies. Those who suffered from the adverse consequences of these ideas were individuals and families seeking help from officially designated experts.

This realization imposes upon practitioners the duty to choose carefully which ideas and practices merit our allegiance, and to be sensitive to the harm that may result from them. This constitutes the generic process of "critical thinking," which encourages us to step outside dominant ways of viewing something and to submit it to logical, ethical, and historical scrutiny (Gibbs & Gambrill, 1999; Paul & Elder, 2002). With respect to developing a critical perspective on the use of psychiatric drugs, helping professionals might wish to reflect on some basic questions. Some of these questions, and answers this author has developed for them so far, follow.

What Does Biological Psychiatry Rest On?

Does the popularity of biological psychiatry rest on its success in providing validated answers to age-old conundrums about mental suffering and healing? For this author, the popularity rests on the simple facts that many people like to use drugs for reasons that are important to them, and that biological psychiatry provides fresh, culturally acceptable justifications for this use (Fancher, 1995). Using drugs to alter consciousness, to ease pain, to induce sleep or maintain wakefulness are universal and ancient practices. Biological psychiatry exploits these ordinary desires with a medical/scientific rhetoric, currently that of the "biochemical imbalance." On radio and on television, in newspaper and magazine articles, and in doctors' offices, people hear, read, and are taught that psychotropic drugs are prescribed for them because their brain functioning is defective. For examples, laypersons and professionals come to believe and repeat that hopelessness and depression result from inadequate serotonin neurotransmission which is remedied by serotonin reuptake inhibitors (Johnson, 1999), or that restlessness and inattention in millions of American school children result from frontal lobe shrinkage and that stimulants help the brain to grow (Kurth, 2002). The reality is of course more complex: people experiencing psychological distress take drugs because they want to, or because others want them to, or because alternatives to drugs are expensive, time-consuming, demanding, and less easily available.

Part of the problem with reductionist biological explanations is that they are commonly presented as obvious scientific facts although *none has been demonstrated* (Mental Health, 1999). In this way, their resemblance to now-discarded dogmas is striking. Earlier explanations, such as the all-powerful but undetectable unconscious, were initially useful to promote professional interests, scientific purposes, and humane reforms. However, as these constructs came to fashion entire societies' outlooks on deviance and distress, they only served to constrain intellectual and therapeutic innovation, and worse (Dolnick, 1998; Torrey, 1992).

How Do Psychotropic Drugs Produce "Therapeutic" Effects?

No single theory in psychopharmacology addresses how drugs produce "therapeutic" effects. Neither the 1090-page *Textbook of*

Psychopharmacology (Schatzberg & Nemeroff, 1998) nor the briefer classic *Primer of Drug Action* (Julien, 1992) discusses any theory of "drug response." This illustrates the unacknowledged fact that the perception of a drug effect as "therapeutic" depends on social context and human motives (Cohen & Karsenty, 1998). How abnormal movements of patients on neuroleptics were initially labeled (or even noticed) depended on expectations of clinicians and inmates in mid-20th century mental hospitals (Cohen, 1997b). Whether sedation from temazepam is called a "main effect" or a "side effect" has nothing to do with the pharmacology of benzodiazepines and everything to do with what participants consider desirable (and at what point in the treatment). Whether indifference and euphoria in a formerly depressed patient taking fluoxetine is labeled as "improvement" or "frontal lobe damage" depends on how long and how closely the patient and the clinician have been interacting (Hoehn-Saric, Lipsey, & McLeod, 1990). Whether submissiveness and cognitive overfocusing in a child taking stimulants is seen as "effectiveness in reducing off-task behavior" or "an expression of the continuum of stimulant toxicity" depends largely on teachers' expectations of children in a structured classroom.

Numerous hypotheses exist to describe how drugs circulate throughout the central nervous system (CNS) and produce cascades of physiological alterations. However, short of postulating a pre-existing (but undetected) "chemical imbalance" that causes undesirable changes in mood and behavior (the "mental disorder"), and that is in turn "corrected" by drugs, the conclusion seems inescapable: most prescribed psychotropics serve as non-selective CNS depressants or stimulants (to use Julien's expression). If that is so, it is unrealistic to expect drugs not to impair or blunt higher human functions including emotional responsiveness, social sensitivity, and judgment. With prolonged use, as the exquisitely integrated brain alters its functioning and structures to adapt to the persistent disruption of neurotransmission by drugs, emotional/cognitive/behavioral/physical impairments can become extremely complex (Breggin & Cohen, 1999). In the extreme, these impairments lead to "iatrogenic denial and helplessness"–a process in which the patient is rendered less independent and discerning, and patient and prescriber work together to deny the damage inflicted (Breggin, 1983).

Pharmacology might indicate how drugs trigger emotional/behavioral states, but it cannot answer questions such as: (1) How do non-specific psychotropic effects come to be desired or shunned, studied or ignored, categorized as "therapeutic" or "adverse"? (2) How and why do conceptions and definitions of therapeutic or adverse effects of particular drugs change over time? (3) How and why might different participants in the prescription situation hold differing views on what should count as a "therapeutic" or "adverse" effect? Some light may be shed on these issues by means of a "person-in-environment" perspective. These issues could be at the core of an independent understanding of medications by social workers.

Does Prescribing Drugs Represent Progress in Mental Healing?

Perhaps the most natural way to comfort someone in distress is to touch that person, or give that person something to swallow. Many professionals might view prescribing or taking a mood-altering drug with the approval of an officially designated helper as a modern or scientific way to treat emotional distress, but the practice can also be seen as a primal custom that resonates with our earliest experiences as powerless infants.

Throughout the ages, recognized and illegitimate healers have used licit and illicit substances to treat all types of ailments. In parallel, sick and distressed people have long claimed benefits from using substances whether or not medical science could validate the claims. For centuries, bleeding was sought by sufferers and administered by physicians. Today, medicine understands bleeding to have been extremely harmful. These examples suggest that: (1) there is nothing inherently progressive or enlightening about the drug treatment of psychological distress; and (2) individuals' experiences of medications as genuine palliatives or curatives illustrate a dimension of healing that may have no reliable relationship to the properties of the particular medications.

What Are Drugs?

Psychotropic drugs are material substances that are ingested inside the body and, according to current ideas in neurophysiology, exert effects on the brain to alter feeling, behaving, and thinking. Drugs' material properties are essential for any understanding of drug effects. Yet, emphasis on material structure impedes discerning much of the significance of drugs in people's lives: their power as *symbols*. From an anthropological perspective, drugs might be seen as "charged objects" (like talismans or amulets) laden by humans with powers, hopes, and fears. Like diamonds reflecting light, the "essence" of medications changes depending on one's standpoint.

Cohen and colleagues (2001) have proposed that medications can appear in numerous forms: (1) the primary strategy to treat disease; (2) an interface between patients and physicians; (3) triggers for personal change, leading some users to radically reinterpret their very sense of self; (4) tools of social control; (5) causes and consequences of medicalization; (6) reservoirs of badness ("dangerous drugs") or goodness ("approved medications") for mainstream society; and (7) vectors of globalization, given how few developed countries sell most of the world's medicines to all the rest of the world's countries. One could characterize medications in other ways, none of which would account for the totality of their effects, but each of which would add to our understanding. In sum, drugs are powerful material objects as well as socially grounded phenomena that are highly responsive to culture and history, producing "effects" that reverberate within and outside individuals' bodies to shape social relations in families, in groups, in institutions, and in societies (Cohen et al., 2001).

Are Some Drugs Better than Others?

From a pharmacological point of view, one cannot explain why various drugs are approved or disapproved, available legally or not, considered beneficial or harmful, promoted or prohibited, available by prescription only or over-the-counter. For example, it is impossible to account for the fates of two stimulants with virtually identical neurochemical effects: methylphenidate (Ritalin) and cocaine (Vastag, 2001). One is prescribed to millions of children, the other is cursed as dangerous for any human being and its mere possession carries heavy legal penalties. Similarly, amphetamines were rejected decades ago by medical and law enforcement authorities as likely to trap users into patterns of substance dependence and to trigger psychosis and violence after prolonged use at high doses (Grinspoon & Hedblom, 1975). Yet today, after antibiotics, the mixture of pure amphetamine salts marketed as Adderall appears to be the drug most prescribed to American children.

These and many other examples suggest that the fate of a psychotropic drug in society has little to do with its known and predictable effects and much to do with how legal and medical authorities choose to treat it. Furthermore, these authorities change their minds frequently on these matters, sometimes every decade. That a drug is approved by the Food and Drug Administration (FDA), prescribed by doctors, promoted by manufacturers, and praised by clinicians and patients says *little* about the drug's "safety" or its "effectiveness." It says even less about how future observers will judge how the medication genuinely impacted those who took it regularly.

Drug Effects: Attributes or Properties?

Students of the history of drug use might observe that various names used to describe or classify drugs are metaphorical and change along with sociocultural transformations. These names may be called attributes: ascribed characteristics or qualities. "Consciousness expanding" (ascribed in the 1960s to "psychedelic" drugs) now stands out as a notable example of a drug attribute. Less obvious but no less valid examples include "antipsychotic," "antidepressant," "mood stabilizer," "cognition enhancer," "addictive," and of course "medication."

Other drug appellations resist linguistic fashion, and may be called "properties." Properties refer to objectively validated drug effects ("sedative," "antiemetic," "anticonvulsant," "myorelaxant," etc.) that pharmacologists usually discover within weeks of systematically screening a given substance for the first time. Properties rarely vary under typical conditions or across different animal species. Undoubtedly, most people, and many experts, confuse attributes and properties. It may be that many individual and societal struggles with drugs stem from a tendency to treat attributes of drugs as if they possessed concrete existence, while neglecting or dismissing the actual properties of drugs.

Drugs or Placebos?

Modern medications are put forth as sophisticated products of rational and technological design, but they cannot detach themselves from their shadow: suggestion. The world's highest enforced scientific and regulatory standards (e.g., those of the FDA) used to classify a compound as an "effective medication" for a given condition may involve nothing more or less than comparing it to a pharmacologically *inert* substance, a placebo. That is because placebos seem to act as vehicles for humans' powerful, innate potential for self-healing and repair.

When primed only with information (including deliberately deceptive information), a person can sincerely report as much or more improvement in symptoms of major depression while taking a yeast pill than while taking a centrally active drug (the composition, effects, dose and administration of which have been studied for years). In re-analyses of the very best clinical trials of seven modern SSRI "antidepressants" (trials submitted to the FDA by manufacturers to gain approval to market the drugs), Kirsch, Moore, Scoboria, and Nichols (2002) have demonstrated barely noticeable advantages of drugs over placebo. Antonuccio, Burns, and Danton (2002) believe that "It could be argued that the patients randomly assigned to placebo are the lucky ones, because they derive a benefit virtually comparable with the medication condition without the associated medical risks." *Mental Health: A Report of the Surgeon General* (1999) states a contrary view: "The evidence for treatment being more effective than placebo is overwhelming" (p. 65). The *Report* does not acknowledge that little evidence exists that any drug used in psychopharmacology will actually surpass an active placebo (a substance that exerts some noticeable physical effects, such as increased heart rate or sweating) in reducing "target symptoms." It may soon become well recognized that, as Fisher and Greenberg (1997) put it for antidepressants (and Thornley and Adams [1998] argued for antipsychotics), "the potency of any [psychotropic medication] is typically inverse to the degree to which the drug trial in which it was tested was adequately controlled" (p. 362).

The placebo effect (simply defined as the patient's expectation) remains possibly the single most important factor in any self-reported positive medication-induced change. However, because it is not directly visible and is completely unpretentious (and unpatentable as placebo), its benefits can easily be claimed by competitors. In the clinical situation, awareness of the placebo effect should compel us to ask how much of a "medication response" truly has anything to do with the "medication."

How Is Knowledge About Drugs Constructed?

The pharmaceutical industry is the most profitable industry in the United States (Fortune, 2000), more than the oil or automobile industries. Like "scientific" knowledge about oil and automobiles, "scientific" knowledge about medications is socially constructed and extremely receptive to the influence of money and power (Safer, 2002; Schulman et al., 2002). Many individuals, failing to discern this system's operations, labor tirelessly and sincerely to concoct inappropriate trial designs, to ignore blatant confounds, to write obscure prose, to publish unfounded claims about the medications they study, and to ignore conflicts of interests. Many journal editors work just as tirelessly to accept these products and pass them off as exemplars of scientific medicine (Relman & Angell, 2002). Other researchers within this system are acutely aware of the bankruptcy of the "business-as-usual" style of psychopharmacotherapy studies but downplay their critical observations, wary of negative repercussions on their careers and livelihoods (Healy, 2002). The activities of other stakeholders and participants in the life cycle of medications, such as manufacturers, regulators, and consumers are also important, if more or less visible.

Under such circumstances, it would be dangerous to believe that the legitimate construction of knowledge about drugs should be the province of officially designated experts. Recently in the case of prescribed psychotropics, and in no small measure because of the advent of the Internet, such knowledge has to accommodate the voices of consumers in areas that psychopharmacologists have consistently ignored or downplayed, such as withdrawal effects (Breggin & Cohen, 1999). This is why it is desirable for a profession professing concern for the powerless to encourage the creation of knowledge among the presumed beneficiaries of drugs, who are often the least powerful in society.

This task takes on increased importance because of the recent return, after six decades of outlawing, of direct-to-consumer advertising of prescription drugs. The modern marketing of Ambien and Adderall, Paxil and Prozac, or Zyban and Zyprexa illustrates that prescribed medications are no longer exclusive tools of medical practice: medications can now be sought or declined on the basis of *consumer preferences.* And, given how such preferences are instilled and shaped in this advanced age of advertising (Cross, 1996) and pharmaceutical industry agenda-setting in mental health (Gosden & Beder, 2001), it is reasonable to expect that in the not-too-distant future, admen, not doctors, will serve as the true intermediaries between us and our drugs.

THE MEDICATION HISTORY FROM A CRITICAL PERSPECTIVE

The preceding discussion hints at some concerns one might have when interviewing a client who takes or considers taking psychotropic medications. These questions should direct practitioners to undertake at least four tasks.

First, they guide practitioners to nourish, as an empowering methodology for their clients and themselves, a critical (questioning, skeptical) attitude toward medications.

Second, they direct practitioners to understand how clients actively construct–through language, expectations, beliefs, and social interaction– their entire medication experience.

Third, they lead practitioners to explore how their clients' medication use interacts with other systems of managing problems and issues in their lives.

Fourth, they suggest that practitioners carefully assess potential adverse effects that prescribers might be prone to miss or dismiss and that clients may sense but may not associate with their medication use.

In addition, from the perspective sketched above, practitioners are urged to take responsibility for their education in medication-related matters. Non-medically trained or psychopharmacologically naive practitioners can be optimistic about their ability to reach novel or useful understandings of medications. How do these suggested tasks of a medication history compare with those discussed in conventional psychiatric literature? A brief analysis of some relevant sources follows.

The Medication History in Psychiatry

A search of the Medline database using the keywords "medication history" yielded only three articles with any relevance to the topic. However, none discussed how such a history should be taken (Gettman, Ranelli, & Ried, 1996; Klungel et al., 2000; Lau, Florax, Porsius, & de Boer, 2000).

Professional or teaching manuals on clinical interviewing constitute another appropriate source of guidelines on taking a psychiatric medication history, and probably no manual better illustrates the current approach in psychiatry than *The Clinical Interview Using DSM-IV-TR–Volume 1: Fundamentals* (Othmer & Othmer, 2002). In it, the "Treatment History" is discussed in a single page of the 547-page volume. The authors identify three purposes of "a detailed history of treatments and treatment responses" (although the discussion focuses almost exclusively on *drug* treatments): "1. . . . to reconstruct what . . . diagnoses another psychiatrist may have entertained if records are not available . . . 2. . . . to help identify responsiveness to certain treatment modalities. . . . 3. . . . to confirm your own diagnosis" (p. 266). A terse clinical example explains each purpose. Here is the entire example for purpose number 2:

> For instance, Keith reports: "I took Wellbutrin for 3 months, and then Serzone for 4 months, and I didn't get any better. My mother went to Dr. J., who switched her from Serzone to Paxil when she didn't respond. Paxil really helped her." Not only disorders but also response to medication may be partly genetically determined.

> Entertain a treatment attempt with a specific serotonin reuptake inhibitor such as paroxetine (Paxil) for a patient like Keith. (p. 266)

For purpose number 3, Othmer and Othmer mention a chronically maladjusted person with periods of increased energy followed by social withdrawal. The clinician notes that the person does not fulfill diagnostic criteria for bipolar disorder and decides to prescribe lithium. Two months later, the patient returns and reports great improvement in his relationships and behavior. Exemplifying the logical fallacy of deducing the nature of a problem from the treatment response, Othmer and Othmer write: "Such a response, even though not treatment specific, may for practical purposes confirm your impression that the patient had a bipolar disorder NOS" (p. 267).

Another expert source touching on the contents of the medication history is entitled *Practical Psychiatric Practice: Forms and Protocols for Clinical Use* (Wyatt, 1998). This manual includes dozens of detailed forms itemizing virtually all possible information from and about patients that psychiatric experts recommend practitioners to collect in order to practice psychiatry. Three different forms are meant to contain information relevant to the patient's history of substance use. In the first, *Self-Assessment Form*, the patient is asked to answer the following question in writing, before the first visit:

> Please describe your illness from the time of your first symptom to the present. Provide as many dates, names and addresses of psychiatrists, psychologists, and/or social workers who have treated you as you can. Also, please provide the kinds of treatment you have received, including names of medications and your response to them. (p. 10)

This same form queries the prospective patient to answer checklist questions about drinking, smoking, and use of illicit drugs. The clinician can choose to record these data, and those obtained from a personal interview, in a second form, the *Initial Psychiatric History and Examination*. It contains a section on the use of caffeine, alcohol, and illicit drugs, but none pertaining to previous prescribed medication use. According to Wyatt, "When completed, the document is a record of the patient's history, mental status examination, the psychiatrist's diagnostic impressions, treatment plans, and recommendations." Of note, "as much as possible, the form was designed to allow the recording of facts with a check mark" (p. 21). The third and final relevant form in Wyatt's volume is the 10-item *Patient (Medication) Information Documentation Form*. It asks the clinician to answer (by checking "yes" or "no") whether the patient, and the patient's family, know "the name(s) of the medication(s) the patient is taking," "what the medication is intended to treat (i.e., the disorder itself or side effects of another medication)," "how to determine if the medication is working," "what to do when a dose is missed," "the name of the disorder for which the patient is seeing you," "the major risks of the disorder and its likely course," "when the patient should take the medication," "how long it should take before they can expect the medication to work," "the most important side effects and what to do when they occur," and "the possible effects of the medication on potentially hazardous activities" (p. 47).

The above sources illustrate that in conventional clinical psychiatry, the over-riding functions of taking a medication history are to help the clinician determine a DSM diagnosis and prescribe a medication. In Othmer and Othmer (2002), the examples of suggested clinical reactions to patients' information deny that psychiatrists are expected to engage in sophisticated or even somewhat individualized biological reasoning when making prescription decisions. In the entire Wyatt (1998) manual, the only question dealing specifically with "medication response" is asked of the patient *in writing*, before the initial visit. Viewed from the critical perspective sketched in this article, these guidelines are superficial and miss the point of taking a medication history of people who seek mental health services. The author would not use these sources as positive pedagogical aids for students, and there is evidence that similar guidelines and training, based on DSM-categorizing and prompt drug treatment, do not impact young residents in psychiatry positively. (For some critical opinions on this matter by psychiatrists, see Kemker & Khadivi, 1995; Smith, 2001; Tucker, 1998; see also Luhrman, 2001). It is difficult to see how such guidelines could help clinicians to reach an understanding of how patients respond to medication, how they interpret its effects, and how medication affects them as biopsychosocial beings. Similarly, it is difficult to see how taking the treatment history within the clinical approach delineated by Othmer and Othmer (2002) and Wyatt (1998) would help patients to make sense of these issues, thus increasing patients' insight, autonomy, and power.

The Psychiatric Medication History: An Interview Schedule

The PMH is designed for use by any helping professional with any clients (except children), in an individual or group format. It may be used for information gathering in the assessment process, in the context of an ongoing counseling or psychotherapeutic relationship, or as a self-help tool for consciousness-raising. Its 30 questions/instructions represent 30 steps in the assessment of medication-related matters, meant to focus on why and how a person uses medication and meant to assist the participants understand the effects (in the biological, psychological, and interpersonal realms) of psychiatric medication. The client's answers can help the practitioner to form opinions on some of the following questions: How is medication "helping" the client? Should the client be referred for specialized assessment to properly diagnose subtle or gross adverse effects? Should the worker consider the possibility that the client would be better off with less of or without the medication? What is the client's potential to undertake a prudent withdrawal? What is the potential of the client's network to support such an endeavor? The PMH is merely one set of guidelines to enter the terrain of medication use and effects: it cannot account for the numerous styles of medication use but it can assist to identify them. What meaning and intelligibility these styles come to have for client and practitioner lies beyond the use of any semi-structured questionnaire.

The overriding task of the person taking such a history is to create a safe space wherein medication-related matters can be examined and discussed without the pressure to diagnose or medicate. A tool such as the PMH is not meant to be used with an involuntary client, as involuntary treatment is inimical to the ideal sort of relationship–voluntary and contractual–that should exist between participants in a helping (educational) encounter. This instrument is not meant to be used in an "emergency" situation, when clients, families, or employers are pressuring practitioners to *do something*. Finally, as discussed in Jacobs and Cohen (1999), there are valid reasons to believe that a proper assessment of medication effects is never complete until the client is able to reflect on the drug experience retrospectively, *from a drug-free standpoint*. Any instrument or interview relying solely on information obtained while the client is medicated will carry this important limitation.

For a practitioner functioning in a multi-disciplinary treatment team that expects a prompt assessment or review of "pertinent facts" in order to dispose of a case, the instrument will be inappropriate. The PMH is probably not meant to be used in a single session, although all the steps can be covered in reasonable detail in a session lasting 75 to 90 minutes. This initial history may be augmented and modified with future probes. During the first interview, the issues are stirred and the client usually raises them later with more curiosity. This links the issues to the client's life, circumstances, problems, strengths, and challenges, and contributes to a proper understanding (assessment) of the client's overall situation. Use of the PMH is not meant to be an end in itself, unless for specific instructional or research purposes clearly explained to the subject and their informed consent obtained. Students in this author's graduate courses regularly use the PMH in course assignments.

Nourishing in clients a critical perspective about medications can be accomplished only if the attitude of the practitioner taking a medication history is one of respect for the client and curiosity about the client's thoughts and beliefs. Neither the most seemingly outlandish responses nor the most "erroneous" interpretations of clients need to be "corrected," at least initially. They can be treated as personal beliefs with which we need not agree but should treat respectfully and, if possible, seek to understand. In the presence of clients in distress, our own prejudices can become blatant, but least of all to ourselves. Thus, respect for and interest in the client's "lived reality" (Farmer and Bentley, 2002) provides the form within which the medication history can properly be taken. One tries to understand this "lived reality" through the client's verbal and non-verbal communications. One might then communicate back to the client what one has understood. One could then engage in a process of gentle challenge of *all* the client's ideas about medication (not simply the ones we find unreasonable), to discover how the client has come to hold them.

Different sections of the PMH explore different themes. Each is briefly discussed below.

Steps 1-3: Baseline. The first three questions on the PMH serve to establish a baseline for the client's problems and idealized solutions. For example, the client has been prescribed medication as a means to suppress painful or undesirable symptoms, to cope with an unpleasant reality. However, the practitioner is led to question whether this solution is uniquely suited to this client's needs, whether it has been implemented after a proper understanding of the clients' context, and whether it incorporates information that the client wished he or she had before undertaking drug treatment. Obtaining clients's present perspective on their difficulties, on what they believe is needed to resolve these difficulties, and on what they see as the main obstacles ahead is done *before* exploring drug-related matters. Indeed, the latter can easily distract or seduce client and helper away from arriving at a fresh understanding of *what is the matter (the problem) and what to do about it from now on.*

After taking the medication history, client and practitioner should find it useful to return to these original questions and to pose them in light of the newer understandings that might have been reached because of the focused exploration of the medication history.

Steps 4-8: Names and instructions. These steps direct the practitioner to list names (including idiosyncratic ones given by the person) and posology of all drugs prescribed/taken, and to gage the person's understanding/memory of the instructions that he or she might have received relative to the taking of medications. This includes asking about which beneficial and adverse effects were mentioned by the prescriber(s) or other health care provider(s). Clients may be asked to bring their medication boxes, bottles, or labels, so that exact information can be obtained. When initially discussing medications, this author has found it useful to have the "actual things" visible. In the peculiar (safe but formal) environment of the consulting office, this paradoxically encourages both an immediacy and a distance from the objects, that is, a perspective, which may otherwise be difficult to create in the abstract.

Step 9: Compliance. This question is meant to gage the person's regularity of drug consumption. Most people do not take medication exactly as prescribed. Individual patterns of consumption vary enormously, and each pattern may have an interesting or revealing justification.

Steps 10-12: First use. These three steps focus the interview on circumstances surrounding the first remembered use of prescribed psychiatric drugs (or the one that the client seems most concerned about). Instances of acute psychological trauma (the sudden loss of a close relative, an episode of psychological or physical abuse, a painful divorce) typically lead people to consult physicians, implicitly or explicitly requesting medications. Whether the consequences of such trauma could or should have been dealt with differently than by a prescription, why they were not, or why other options were tried and abandoned are questions of interest. With prolonged drug use, various other problems, including drug-induced problems, may have papered over the initial difficulties. How drugs actually made a difference during the initial crisis, how this was evaluated, and for what reason they are still taken weeks, months, or years after the initial crisis are critical matters that require exploration.

In contrast to the clinical psychiatric suggestions reviewed in the previous section of this article, the client's DSM labels are not of interest here, besides providing some idea why other clinicians might have prescribed a certain medication. DSM labels cannot make up for the first-person story, which connects events, circumstances and history *from the person's perspective* to the person's emotions, thoughts and actions (Jacobs & Cohen, in press).

Steps 13-19: Effects. This section guides the practitioner to ask general and specific questions concerning what and how the client thinks the medication(s) is affecting him or her. One should cover at least as many areas (physical, cognitive, emotional, practical, social) as are suggested, because unless queried specifically most people do not typically make connections between their medication use and various emotional and behavioral states. Depending on the practitioner's level of knowledge of how drugs impact the body and how bodily organs impact drugs, questions can focus on some of these issues. Conversely, depending on the client's answers and the practitioner's knowledge and observations, other questions can explore medications' effects on processes such as emotion regulation, social sensitivity, short- and long-term memory, attentiveness to detail, ability to monitor one's psychological state, and concern for other people. Two additional questions ask the client to name any distinctive (characteristic, singular) psychological and physical effects of the medications. For example, some people taking "antidepressants" or "mood stabilizers" would not describe their distinctive psychological effects in these words, if asked in the context described above. These queries help clients to use their own language to produce a more "valid" (i.e., experience-tested) description of the medication.

Steps 20-21: Non-drug solutions. Here, the person is asked to describe other informal and formal attempts, besides taking prescribed medication, that may have been pursued to solve their problems: how serious were the attempts, what were the results, and what lessons were learned.

Steps 22-26: Drug withdrawal. Whether examined from a pharmacological, emotional, psychological, or familial angle, the issue of withdrawal from psychiatric drugs remains complex. The effects some people experience when they stop taking their medications, or merely reduce the dosage, or skip a few doses can be the most significant of their entire drug taking episode. However, such withdrawal effects are not acknowledged by many practitioners, and even less so in the published literature. What is more, unpleasant effects which are likely to abate with a truly gradual taper of medications may be described to patients by health professionals as evidence that the patient "needs" to remain on the medications indefinitely. Because many stakeholders in the mental health system are invested ideologically and emotionally in a view of medications as the essential intervention, rational discussions about drug withdrawal rarely take place. Nevertheless, they may rank highly on clients' agendas. In sum, an "unbiased" discussion of the client's experience of stopping to take medications and reinstituting them should be an integral part of any medication related discussion.

Steps 27-29: Social network. These questions are aimed to understand to what degree the client's current medication use might respond or conform to, or fail to meet, others' expectations, especially family members, friends, and health professionals. Question 29 asks the client to describe the last three different conversations about his or her medication use.

CONCLUSION

Clients seeking or receiving mental health services today have many reasons to be wary of the *zeitgeist* of the times. From this author's perspective, there have been several worrying developments during the last two decades: rampant biologization of distress; overemphasis of drug treatments at the expense of every other sort of intervention; increasing adoption by psychologists and social workers of biomedical models of categorizing distress and intervening with clients; decreasing privacy within the therapeutic relationship; and increasing social acceptance of involuntary psychiatric interventions. These and other trends highlight the importance of creating safe spaces where clients and practitioners can critically explore the issue of psychiatric medications.

For clients, discussing their medication use along the guidelines suggested in this article could provide an opportunity to construct an independent, evidence-tested personal narrative about their drug-taking. It could serve to uncover some otherwise unarticulated impacts of medications on their lives, including the extent of psychological alterations brought about by centrally acting substances. It could help to clarify their representations of medications, medication effects, and mechanisms of drug action, as well as the origins of these representations. It could help them to discern how taking medications might be structuring some of their interpersonal relationships and activities, and how, in turn, these relationships influence their medication use. It could assist in articulating clients' desire to stop taking medication and entertain other options to manage their distress.

For practitioners, the PMH offers a person-in-environment point of entry into the psychopharmacology scene. Conducting ten or more of these in-depth histories with different clients will provide any social worker, regardless of their current knowledge level, with a wealth of information and hypotheses about the social and behavioral effects of psychotropic medications. Much of this information is simply unavailable in published works. This information can be systematized, tested, and shared with colleagues and students. Taking a psychiatric medication history can help practitioners to understand their clients' experiences and can assist clients to develop conscious ways to integrate or exclude psychiatric medication from their lives.

REFERENCES

Antonuccio, D. O., Burns, D. D., & Danton, W. G. (2002). Antidepressants: A triumph of marketing over science? *Treatment and Prevention, 5,* article 25. Available on World Wide Web, http://journals.apa.org/prevention/volume5/pre0050025c.html

Braslow, J. (1997). *Mental ills and bodily cures: Psychiatric treatment in the first half of the twentieth century.* Berkeley: University of California Press.

Breggin, P. R. (1983). Iatrogenic helplessness in authoritarian psychiatry. In R. F. Morgan (Ed.), *The iatrogenics handbook: A critical look at research and practice in the helping professions* (pp. 39-51). Toronto: IPI Publishing.

Breggin, P.R., & Cohen, D. (1999). *Your drug may be your problem: How and why to stop taking psychiatric medications.* Cambridge, MA: Perseus.

Cohen, D. (1988). Social work and psychotropic drug treatments. *Social Service Review, 62,* 576-599.

Cohen, D. (1997a). A critique of the use of neuroleptic drugs in psychiatry. In S. Fisher & R. G. Greenberg (Eds.), *From placebo to panacea: Putting psychiatric drugs to the test* (pp. 173-228). New York: Wiley.

Cohen, D. (1997b). Psychiatrogenics: Introducing chlorpromazine in psychiatry. *Review of Existential Psychology and Psychiatry, 23* (1-2), 206-233.

Cohen, D. (2001). How to detoxify from common illusions about psychiatric medications. *Ethical Human Sciences and Services, 3,* 207-211.

Cohen, D. (2002). Research on the drug treatment of schizophrenia: A critical appraisal and implications for social work education. *Journal of Social Work Education, 38,* 217-239.

Cohen, D., Collin, J., Perodeau, G., & McCubbin, M. (2001). Medications as social phenomena. *Health: An Interdisciplinary Journal for the Social Study of Health, Illness and Medicine, 5,* 441-469.

Cohen, D., & Jacobs, D. (2000). A model consent form for psychiatric drug treatment. *Journal of Humanistic Psychology, 40,* 59-64.

Cohen, D., & Karsenty, S. (1998). Représentations sociales des effets secondaires des anxiolytiques: Une étude comparative Québec-France. [Social representations of the side effects of anxiolytic drugs: A comparative Quebec-France study]. Research report submitted to the Research Branch, Ministry of Health & Municipal Affairs, France.

Cross, M. (1996). (Ed). *Advertising and culture: Theoretical perspectives*. Westport, CT: Praeger.

Dolnick, E. (1998). *Madness on the couch: Blaming the victim in the heyday of psycho-analysis*. New York: Simon & Schuster.

Fancher, R. T. (1995). *Cultures of healing: Correcting the image of American mental health care*. San Francisco: Freeman.

Farmer, R., & Bentley, K. J. (2002). Social workers as medication facilitators. In K. J. Bentley (Ed.), *Social work practice in mental health: Contemporary roles, tasks, and techniques* (pp. 211-229). Pacific Grove, CA: Brooks/Cole.

Fisher, S., & Greenberg, R. G. (1997). What are we to conclude about psychoactive drugs? In S. Fisher & R. Greenberg (Eds.), *From placebo to panacea: Putting psychiatric drugs to the test* (pp. 359-384). New York: Wiley.

Floersch, J. (2002). *Meds, money, and manners: The case management of severe mental illness*. New York: Columbia University Press.

Fortune. (2000). How the industries stack up. Retrieved October 17, 2000, from http://www.fortune.com/indexw.jhtml?channel=artcol.jhtml&doc_id=00001423

Gettman, D. A., Ranelli, P. L., & Ried, L.D. (1996). Influence of gender on outcomes of medication-history interviewing. *Patient Education and Counseling, 27*, 147-160.

Gibbs, L., & Gambrill, E. (1999). *Critical thinking for social workers: Exercises for the helping professions*. Thousand Oaks, CA: Pine Forge Press.

Gosden, R., & Beder, S. (2001). Pharmaceutical agenda-setting in mental health policy. *Ethical Human Sciences and Services, 3*, 147-159.

Grinspoon, L., & Hedblom, P. (1975). *The speed culture: Amphetamine use and abuse in America*. Cambridge, MA: Harvard University Press.

Healy, D. (1997). *The antidepressant era*. Cambridge, MA: Harvard University Press.

Healy, D. (2002, February). *Problems with antidepressants*. Paper presented at the Institute of Psychiatry, London.

Hoehn-Saric, R., Lipsey, J. R., & McLeod, D. A. (1990). Apathy and indifference in patients on fluvoxamine and fluoxetine. *Journal of Clinical Psychopharmacology, 10*, 343-345.

Jacobs, D. H., & Cohen, D. (1999). What is really known about psychological alterations produced by psychiatric drugs? *International Journal of Risk and Safety in Medicine, 12*, 37-47.

Jacobs, D. H., & Cohen, D. (In press). Hidden in plain sight: DSM-IV's rejection of the categorical approach to psychiatric diagnosis. *Review of Existential Psychology and Psychiatry*.

Johnson, A. B. (1990). *Out of Bedlam: The truth about deinstitutionalization*. New York: Basic Books.

Johnson, H. C. (1999). *Psyche, synapse, and substance: The role of neurobiology in emotion, behavior, thinking, and addiction for non-scientists*. Greenfield, MA: Deerfield Valley.

Julien, R. M. (1992). *A primer of drug action: A concise, nontechnical guide to the actions, uses, and side effects of psychoactive drugs* (6th ed.). New York: Freeman.

Kemker, S. S., & Khadivi, A. (1995). Psychiatric education: Learning by assumption. In C. Ross & A. Pam (Eds.), *Pseudoscience in biological psychiatry: Blaming the body* (pp. 241-253). New York: Wiley.

Kirsch, I., Moore, T. J., Scoboria, A., & Nicholls, S. N. (2002). The Emperor's new drugs: An analysis of antidepressant medication data submitted to the U.S. Food and Drug Administration. *Prevention & Treatment, 5*, article 23. Available on World Wide Web: http://journals.apa.org/prevention/volume5/toc-jul15-02.htm

Klungel, O. H., de Boer, A., Paes, A. H. P., Herings, R. M. C., Seidell, J. C., & Bakker, A. (2000). Influence of question structure on the recall of self-reported drug use. *Journal of Clinical Epidemiology, 53*, 273-277.

Kurth, J. (2002, December 12). Ritalin is safe–and it works. *The Detroit Free Press.* Retrieved December 12, 2002, from http://www.detnews.com

Lau, H. S., Florax, C., Porsius, A. J., & de Boer, A. (2000). The completeness of medication histories in hospital medical records of patients admitted to general internal medicine wards. *British Journal of Clinical Pharmacology, 49*, 597-603.

Luhrman, T. M. (2001). *Of two minds: The growing disorder in American psychiatry.* New York: Knopf.

Mental health: A report of the Surgeon General. (1999). Rockville, MD: Department of Health and Human Services.

Othmer, E., & Othmer, S. C. (2002). *The clinical interview using DSM-IV-TR. Volume 1: Fundamentals.* Washington, D.C. & London: American Psychiatric Press.

Paul, R. W., & Elder, L. (2002). *Critical thinking: Tools for taking charge of your professional and personal life.* Upper Saddle River, NJ: Financial Times/Prentice Hall.

Relman, A., & Angell, M. (2002, December 16). America's other drug problem: How the drug industry distorts medicine and politics. *The New Republic.* Retrieved December 19, 2002 from http://www.tnr.com

Research Triangle Institute. (2002). *Screening for depression: Systematic evidence review.* Rockville, MD: Agency for Health Care Quality and Research.

Safer, D. J. (2002). Design and reporting modifications in industry-sponsored comparative psychopharmacology trials. *Journal of Nervous and Mental Disease, 190*, 583-592.

Schatzberg, A. F., & Nemeroff, C. (Eds.). (1998). *The American Psychiatric Press textbook of psychopharmacology* (2nd ed.). Washington, DC: American Psychiatric Press.

Schulman, K. A., Seils, D. M., Timbie, J. W., Sugarman, J., Dame, L. A., Weinfurt, K. P., Mark, D. B., & Califf, R. M. (2002). A national survey of provisions in clinical-trial agreements between medical schools and industry sponsors. *New England Journal of Medicine, 347*, 1335-1341.

Smith, D. (2001). On the incompatibility of the biological and empathic-relational model. *Ethical Human Sciences and Services, 3*, 47-52.

Thornley, B., & Adams, C. (1998). Content and quality of 2000 controlled trials in schizophrenia over 50 years. *British Medical Journal, 317*, 1181-1184.

Torrey, E. F. (1992). *Freudian fraud: The malignant impact of Freud's theory on American thought and culture.* New York: HarperCollins.

Tucker, G. (1998). Putting DSM-IV in perspective. *American Journal of Psychiatry, 155*, 159-161.

Vastag, B. (2001). Pay attention: Ritalin acts much like cocaine. *JAMA, 286*, 905-906.

Whitaker, R. (2002). *Mad in America: Bad science, bad medicine, and the enduring mistreatment of the mentally ill.* Cambridge, MA: Perseus Publishing.

Wyatt, R. J. (1998). *Practical psychiatric practice: Forms and protocols for clinical use* (2nd ed.). Washington, D.C. & London: American Psychiatric Press.

Zito, J. M., Safer, D. J., dosReis, S., Gardner, J. F., Magder, L., Soeken, K., Boles, M., Lynch, F., & Riddle, M. (2003). Psychotropic practice patterns for youth: A 10-year perspective. *Archives of Pediatric and Adolescent Medicine, 157,* 17-25.

The Psychology
of the Psychopharmacology Triangle:
The Client, the Clinicians,
and the Medication

Sarah S. Bradley

SUMMARY. The psychopharmacological triangle generated by recent changes in mental health practices requires social workers to deepen their understanding of the psychological meanings of such treatment. Many clients receive concurrent psychotherapeutic and psychopharmacological interventions from different providers, creating a triangular treatment relationship. To facilitate a successful outcome, social workers will need to understand how meaning, transference and countertransference are stimulated by this arrangement. The literature on these issues as well as clinical experience will highlight specific issues requiring attention. By attending to these dynamics, the social worker can maximize the chances for a successful treatment outcome. *[Article copies available for a fee from The Haworth Document Delivery Service: 1-800-HAWORTH. E-mail address: <docdelivery@haworthpress.com> Website: <http://www.HaworthPress.com> © 2003 by The Haworth Press, Inc. All rights reserved.]*

KEYWORDS. Collaboration, managing meaning, referral

The original version of this paper was initially presented at the First National Internet Conference on Social Work and Psychopharmacology, February 3-24, 2003, sponsored by the Ittleson Foundation and the Virginia Commonwealth University School of Social Work in association with Psy Broadcasting Company.

[Haworth co-indexing entry note]: "The Psychology of the Psychopharmacology Triangle: The Client, the Clinicians, and the Medication." Bradley, Sarah S. Co-published simultaneously in *Social Work in Mental Health* (The Haworth Social Work Practice Press, an imprint of The Haworth Press, Inc.) Vol. 1, No. 4, 2003, pp. 29-50; and: *Psychiatric Medication Issues for Social Workers, Counselors, and Psychologists* (ed: Kia J. Bentley) The Haworth Social Work Practice Press, an imprint of The Haworth Press, Inc., 2003, pp. 29-50. Single or multiple copies of this article are available for a fee from The Haworth Document Delivery Service [1-800-HAWORTH, 9:00 a.m. - 5:00 p.m. (EST). E-mail address: docdelivery@haworthpress.com].

Digital Object Identifier: 10.1300/J200v01n04_03

INTRODUCTION

Mental health care in the United States has changed dramatically in the last 15 years and social workers have become an integral part of that change (Cohen, 2003). By 1995 social workers made up 23% of the clinically trained mental health having become significant partners in the treatment process with clients, families and prescriber personnel (Manderscheid & Sonnenschein, 1996). Over the last 20 years mental health practice has been greatly influenced by the refinement of diagnostic criteria and the exponential increase in the usage of psychiatric medications to treat these illnesses (Bentley & Walsh, 2001). Concurrently, managed care has forced changes on the mental health delivery system, increasing the involvement of social work practitioners and leading to tensions between practitioners (Cohen, 2003). Despite this increase in nonmedical practitioners, the system of care remains based on a medical model in which diagnosis and rapid return of functioning are the primary goals. Psychiatry is primarily focused on the biological nature of mental illness and increasingly relying on the utilization of pharmacological interventions (Gabbard & Kay, 2001). Despite this focus, Gabbard and Kay note that a large majority of clients still remain in combined psychotherapy and pharmacotherapy, but nonmedical practitioners are providing this treatment. If we expand this to include those receiving pharmacotherapy and other psychosocial treatments, this percentage would clearly grow. Social workers, as providers of 65% of all the psychotherapy and mental health services in this country, are influenced by these changes and intricately involved in managing the resulting treatment configurations (Gibelman & Schervich, 1997).

These treatment configurations take the form of a psychopharmacological triangle–the client, the clinicians and the medications. This triangle is influence by the psychology of all partners and the unique characteristics of the medication, its dosing and side effects. The relationships between the partners and the treatment outcome are impacted by the historical and cultural context of the treatment, the beliefs and meaning about illness and treatment, and transference and countertransference. To maximize outcome, social workers need to attend to these multiple influences. Specifically, how in the context of the therapeutic relationship can we understand the individual stories and meanings that are constructed by clients, their families, and their treatment providers around illness and medications?

OUTCOME AND MEANING

Successful outcome is not solely a matter of matching the right medication with the right diagnosis, but is a multivariate process. Psychotherapy outcome research suggests that positive outcome is impacted by relationship factors, specifically feelings of "trust, warmth, acceptance, and human wisdom" (Lambert, 1994, p. 181). Outcome in addiction treatment is impacted by the motivation to change as delineated by the stage system of change (Prochaska, Diclemente, & Norcross, 1992). This stage system notes where on a motivational continuum a client falls and addresses the intervention to that level of motivation. Recently this model has been applied to issues related to compliance with medical treatments (Butler, Rollnick, & Stott, 1996). Finally, placebo, hope, and expectation for change all impact psychotherapy outcome (Miller, Duncan, & Hubble, 1997). The placebo effect has been demonstrated to be a biological phenomenon, partially influenced by clients' positive expectations (Brown University Child and Adolescent Psychopharmacology Update, 2002). Examining these factors and looking beyond the language differences, there are commonalities in what this data say about outcome. These observations suggest there is something about the client's beliefs and expectations, locus for change, treatment modality, and treatment relationship that impacts outcome. These factors are reflected clinically in the stories and metaphors clients construct about their illness, its treatment and their relationships with the treatment providers.

Individuals construct stories and thus meaning by integrating different affective and relational experiences, memories, behavior, and cognitive schema. These metaphors are deconstructed through exploration of the real as well as transferential and countertransferential reactions to illness, treatment and treatment providers. Parallel to client generated metaphors are those metaphors generated by clinicians. These metaphors similarly reflect the clinicians own conscious and unconscious processes. Social workers need to attend to how the experience of the self and the multiple relationships impact the stories and meaning that are constructed around treatment. These issues become increasingly complex when clients are seen in the psychopharmacological treatment triangle. This triangular relationship, consisting of the client, social worker, and prescriber provides fertile ground for the generation of multiple and potentially competing beliefs and attitudes.

Addressing these issues in the context of the pharmacological treatment triangle can have significant impact on the outcome of treatment.

In order to accomplish this, social workers must explore how transference and countertransference within this treatment configuration can promote or impede treatment. There are two points along the treatment continuum that are particularly critical to examine: the point at which one makes the referral for a medication consultation, and the point of medication initiation. While psychotherapy is the most commonly discussed treatment modality integrated with pharmacotherapy, one is encouraged to expand the psychopharmacology triangle to include the multiple collaborative roles engaged in by social workers in mental health. Providing case management, psychoeducation, vocational rehabilitation and counseling produces the same triangular treatment relationships and requires the same level of sophisticated reflection and understanding.

The terms transference and countertransference will be used in their more modern relational sense. Traditionally, they have been used to describe unconscious, unresolved neurotic conflicts based on earlier experiences. Countertransference was thought to hinder the treatment process and thus was to be eliminated. They are now conceptualized as both unconscious material generated by the client and the clinician as well as conscious experiences that resonate from the real relationship (Delacour, 1996). Both transference and countertransference impact the meaning and metaphors that are constructed by clients and mental health providers, and understanding this can provide a window into some of the factors impacting outcome.

TO REFER OR NOT TO REFER?

An important juncture for social workers providing therapy is reached when a decision is made to refer or not to refer for psychopharmacology. The social worker needs clarity around the diagnosis, the efficacy of medications, the client's goals and beliefs about illness and treatment, and the purpose of the consultation. Additionally, there are unconscious factors that may impact the social worker's decision to refer. Whether this idea is generated by the client or the social worker, one must address "why now?" How do beliefs about illness and transference and countertransference impact the decision? What affective responses does this process generate? Gould and Busch (1998) note that client responses to medication referrals "run the gamut from relief to panic, to anger and depression" (p. 732), and a parallel process is generated in the social worker. This decision has to be understood in the context of the treatment relationship with an appreciation of the power of unconscious processes.

Client and the Medication Referral

Clients and families requesting treatment for mental health problems bring with them beliefs about causation and parallel ideas about treatment. If social workers believe the research that states our beliefs about illnesses and treatment are as powerful as the actual interventions, then it is important to listen for these issues (Miller et al., 1997). Clients experience their problems in multiple ways: as moral failures or character weaknesses, as externally caused, as biological or psychological defects, as intolerable feeling states or as impairments in functioning. For some the symptomatology becomes symbolic, having meaning for the self and one's place in the world. Similar beliefs and expectations evolve around treatment, including changing the environment, psychological growth, biological interventions, symptom reduction, functionality and cure vs. regulation of illness. All of these beliefs about the illness and treatment have ramifications for what actually happens in the treatment and, ultimately, the outcome.

A referral for medications would probably be consistent with the beliefs of a client who felt they had a "chemical imbalance," but what about others? There are other clients for whom a medication referral may create anxiety, depression, or rage. A client for whom insight and psychological struggle are a valued part of the treatment process may experience a referral for medications as a narcissistic assault. They may construe this to mean they are too sick for psychological treatments. A client with hypomanic symptoms may find the increased energy, productivity and grandiosity quite functional and perceive the difficulty as being relational and the medication referral a threat (Nevins, 1990). The client with psychotic symptoms may find the voices comforting or organizing and thus medication threatens this stability (Hoge & Guthiel, 1989). Clients for whom depressive symptoms serve as a mechanism for maintaining an attachment with a depressed parent may have their sense of self threatened (Fenton, Blyler, & Heinssen, 1997). Masi, Marcheschi, and Luccherino (1996) note that clients may similarly experience the "depressive symptoms as the only vital content that can fill their psychic emptiness and affective anesthesia" (p. 928). They note adolescents struggling to balance needs for independence and dependence may experience medications as a threat to this balance. Additionally, how might suggesting a medication consult impact a client who believes their illness is the result of moral weakness or external factors?

Identifying client's beliefs about illness as they relate to the medication referral can have a powerful impact on outcome. When beliefs about illness or treatment are not compatible with a biological model, a referral for psychopharmacology may have unintended consequences. A medication referral for these clients can result in their leaving treatment; passively complying in order to please the social worker, restricting information about symptoms in subsequent sessions or not adhering to the treatment as prescribed. All of which can have a negative impact on treatment adherence and outcome.

When the request for medication is client generated it is worth considering the unconscious motivating factors. Clearly there are cultural and social factors that may lead a client to request medications. There are also unconscious factors relate to both the self and the therapeutic relationship that may lead to a request for medications.

Masi et al. (1996) note the potential for a medication request to be a defensive attempt to protect the stability of self, by diverting attention away from the psychological self as acknowledging intrapsychic issues is too painful. Lurie (1991) identifies a medication request as a possible defensive maneuver in which "externalization or somatization, removes responsibility and conflict from the patients as agents of their lives and places it in their brains" (p. 349). A medication request may externalize the locus of control allowing the client to safeguard his or her own sense of self or signal that the current affective state is so foreign and intolerable that it requires immediate removal. Identifying these issues can provide a richer appreciation of the client's internal and external world and allow for the client and social worker to address components of these reactions that interfere with the treatment process.

The request for medication can also be understood in the context of the therapeutic relationship. A request for a medication consultation may be a form of triangulation in which the client attempts to decrease anxiety brought on by closeness and/or conflict with the social worker (Nevins, 1990). Are there issues in the transference that have been activated by treatment and the medication request is an attempt to gain some distance and focus on more concrete and conscious material? Some clients may become anxious in response to increasing attachment to the social worker and the medications are an attempt to provide distance. Other clients for whom conflict is particularly difficult may request medication as a way of avoiding conflict in the treatment relationship. For some, the request for medication may be a disguised attempt at terminating treatment or indirectly criticizing the social worker. Thus the request for medications can be understood as an attempt to use another clinician or medication to manage the real and transferential aspects of therapeutic relationship.

The decision by the social worker not to refer for a psychopharmacological evaluation carries just as powerful meanings for the client. It can signal a belief in the client's capacity to self-manage or the social worker's capacity to heal (Dewan, 1992). It can mean the illness is not serious and thereby solidify a dyadic pact against the illness. The client's request for medications may be a test and the social worker's refusal to make a referral can be evidence that the social worker is "incorruptible" and can't be "sidetracked" (Hoge and Guthiel, 1989). On the negative, the decision not to refer can be experienced sadistically as the social worker withholding a cure or punishing the client (Dewan, 1992). The social worker can be seen as protecting their turf, being afraid to share the client or the treatment, or threatened by the client's autonomy. Clients may feel guilty for asking, deducing that no referral means the social worker doubts the seriousness of their concerns (Hoge & Guthiel, 1989). Clearly these responses will have implications for the ongoing treatment relationship and the treatment progress and lead us again to ask, "what does it mean if I refer or don't refer?" Pondering this and the other questions won't necessarily give one an answer, but it allows for a broader view of the multitude of client factors that can impact this decision. This view can deepen our understanding of the client and enhance the ongoing relationship and, hopefully, the outcome.

Social Worker and the Medication Referral

The social worker's own beliefs about and reactions to the illness, the client and the treatment parallel the client's responses to the decision to refer or not to refer for a medication consultation. Theoretical practice models, historical and cultural contexts, as well as our countertransferential responses to clients and their illnesses impact the beliefs and meanings that we construct around these issues. Exploring some of these factors and acknowledging their presence will allow for a dialogue about their potential influences.

Social workers practice from a biopsychosocial perspective, but choose their own model of practice, which is conceptualized on top of a theoretical framework. Some embrace theoretical models that explain problems in intrapsychic, behavioral, familial, environmental, systemic, or cognitive terms. Many of these theories then suggest specific therapeutic interventions to address the problem and promote change (Payne, 1997). In addition to these interventions, we integrate other models of intervention that have differential points of attention and intervention (Sheafor & Horejsi, 2003). Within the social work field, as well as in mental health in general, the integration of traditional social work practice frameworks and the pharmacological revolution has generated significant controversy (Bentley & Walsh, 2001; Klerman, 1991). Social workers pondering a referral for a medication consultation need to be conscious of how their beliefs and theoretical frameworks impact why, when and how this decision is made. A rigid adherence to any biological, psychological, or social model of practice may obscure our ability to practice competently and compassionately. As with all beliefs, caution is needed in exclusively embracing any one framework or explanation. Social workers must critically address the benefits that derive from various viewpoints and integrate these with the client's beliefs about health and illness into a truly biopsychosocial perspective.

There is a lure to polarize the medication debate into an either/or, right/wrong, or good/evil conflict. This battle has historical, cultural, legal, economic, and social roots (Bradley, 1990; Nevins, 1990) causing those who believe and those who don't to constantly attempt to disprove the other. Since the 60s, research has underscored the biological components of mental illness, and psychiatry programs have increasingly embraced this focus. Gabbard and Kay (2001) argue this pendulum swing in psychiatry has been at the expense of an integrated biopsychosocial perspective and notes there are continued pressures toward "biological reductionism." This split may reflect an attempt to defend against the anxiety brought on by the complexities of mental health problems and treatment. "Biological reductionism may appeal to all of us when immersing ourselves in human suffering is too much to bear" and medications offer "an illusion of mastery over complexities of psychiatric illness" (Gabbard & Kay, 2001, p. 1959). Conversely, rigid adherence to nonbiological models and expecting the client and/or social worker alone to address these complexities may appeal to grandiose fantasies of omnipotent control and self-reliance and serve as a mechanism for self-validation and/or a defense against a sense of powerlessness. Engaging in this polarization negates one of the foundations of social work, the biopsychosocial nature of our clients, their problems, and the solutions. While social work has attempted to maintain a balanced perspective, this shift in psychiatry has put tremendous pressure on the collaborative treatment relationship and can unconsciously impact the relationship between different disciplines.

Other societal pressures can insert themselves into a decision about medication referrals. Managed care has developed practice standards that commonly reflect a biological bias and focus solely on symptom reduction. In some cases, psychopharmacology has been required if reimbursement is to continue, regardless of the client's or social worker's perspective. At the same time, the majority of providers are nonphysicians and so triangular treatment relationships are the norm (Manderscheid & Sonnenschein, 1996). Often this collaboration is not by choice. Meyer and Simon (1999a) call this "a clinical shotgun wedding" (p. 244). This type of forced partnership also exists in clinic settings where social workers have little choice about with which prescriber to share their clients. As with any involuntary relationship this can lead to less than optimal collaboration. Legal pressures have also raised anxiety about relying solely on psychosocial interventions (Nevins, 1990). "Evidence-based practice" standards have become the standard of care by which one will be judged if having to defend one's practice in court, and these standards are predominantly biological in nature. Uncritically embracing these standards and externally derived mandates risks eliminating the relational, social, and psychological nature inherent in a biopsychosocial practice.

Having addressed professional issues that impact a referral for medications, one needs to look at how relational responses, real and countertransferential, to clients and their illnesses impact this decision (Nevins, 1990). Awareness of this raises some questions to be asked when contemplating a referral. Nevins (1990) and Rubin (2001) encourage one to think about how the thought of making a referral is impacted by countertransference to components of the illness or the client. Specifically, how does the fragmented, chaotic, empty, primitive experience of the client with schizophrenia impact us? Who are we treating when we think about referring the dependent, apathetic client with depression? What does the grandiose, belligerent, sexual, elated client activate in us? How do we metabolize the psychic and physical trauma of the client with PTSD? How does countertransference to the hateful, labile, idealizing/devaluing client impact our decision? Finally, who is being treated when we refer the client with anxiety for anxiolytics? There is a risk of prematurely responding to the dependent, apathetic client with a directive, authoritarian medication referral in order to relieve tension for both the client and the social worker (Nevins, 1990). There is a risk of using a medication referral as retaliation to the hateful client, or responding to the fragmented client with a premature medication referral based on our need for cohesion and integration. The social worker working with clients with trauma histories has to be alert to the difficulties in containing the shame, guilt, and rage and not using the medication referral as a vehicle for acting out the need to be in the savior role (Southwick & Yehuda, 1993). Nevins (1990) calls these reactions the "evocative pull" (p. 327) in response to the client's unconscious material, and our reaction "medical countertransference" (p. 328).

In some cases the process by which we do or don't refer for a psychopharmacological consultation may reflect countertransferential issues related to our attachment styles (Gould & Busch, 1998; Rubin, 2001; Kelly, 1992). Clearly social workers have character and attachment styles that reflect those in the general population and these styles impact how we respond to the medication issue. A social worker whose sense of self is narcissistically involved in the outcome of the treatment may experience the lack of response to psychotherapy or psychosocial treatments as an assault on the self. The medication referral, in this case, may be a defensive act that underscores the failure as residing in the client, not in the treatment. The anxious and insecure social worker may experience shame and humiliation in regard to lack of progress and fear the referral will expose their work and their status as not a legitimate "doctor" (Kelly, 1992). The anxious and ambivalent social worker may view the medication referral as a sign of nurturing when in fact it is a mechanism for acting out rescue fantasies and avoiding conflict (Rubin, 2001). The more detached social worker may initiate a medication referral as a mechanism for maintaining distance when issues in the transference are overwhelming. The referral thus conveys to the client the idea that feelings are unacceptable, needing to be medicated away or taken to a different "doctor." In response to being overwhelmed, the more disorganized social worker may idealize the medications or use a referral as a means of treating their own affective states or conversely not make a referral because the medication is viewed as a powerful, dangerous competitor (Hyland, 1991).

From the previous discussion one can appreciate the myriad trouble spots that can arise when a social worker contemplates a referral for a medication evaluation or reevaluation. There may be conflicts between belief systems about illness and treatment that lead to differential goals for treatment. There may be unresolved historical or cultural influences that skew the social worker's perspective. The character and attachment styles of social worker and client impact the decision to refer and the meaning of that referral. The source of the initiation and the manifestations of the illness all have implications for the referral and consequently the future course of the treatment itself. By consciously reflecting on these multiple dynamics one has the opportunity, when appropriate, to explore them with the client. This dialogue, both internal and external, allows for a greater appreciation of the complexities of the treatment relationship and enhances clients' capacities to maximize treatment opportunities. This also sets the stage for the social worker's ongoing involvement with the initiation and maintenance stages of psychopharmacology. In this way a referral for medications can be based on an understanding of the client, the diagnosis, and the relevance of biological interventions instead of attempts to distance, organize, or punish clients and/or alleviate one's own uncomfortable affective states.

MEDICATION INITIATION
AND THE TRIANGULAR TREATMENT RELATIONSHIP

The clinical relationships become exceedingly complicated when medications are initiated because a triangular treatment relationship develops. If we are to achieve optimal outcome, the multiple relationships within this triangle require attention. Each member of the triangle is dyadically involved with every other member as well as with the medication, which creates three therapeutic triangles. The client is in a relationship with two clinicians, social worker and prescriber. This requires awareness of how the beliefs, historical conflicts, and transference and countertransference reactions impact the metaphorical meanings of these relationships. The client and each clinician are also in a triangular relationship with at least one medication. Beliefs about medications and illness may impact the thoughts and feelings about a specific medication, the dosage, the side effects and/or the therapeutic response. These responses are mediated by past experience with medication as well as transference to medication. While transference is usually an unconscious process between individuals, Hoge and Guthiel (1989) conceptualize medications as being potential transference objects. These are manifested, in the medications being the focus of idealization, fantasy, displacement and symbolization. It is thus necessary to understand the clients' and clinicians' responses to each other and the medications. The risk is that without awareness of these psychological issues, splits and alliances can develop which impede successful integration of all biopsychosocial aspects of the client's experience and negatively impact outcome.

Client Within the Therapeutic Triangle

The client's positive and negative transferential responses to the medications as well as to the two clinicians need examining as they have important implications for outcome. Both positive and negative transference reactions occur and have an impact on the sense of self and the therapeutic alliance. Transference reactions that reflect experiences of self are qualitatively different from those that are relational and require different therapeutic responses.

Positive Transference

Positive transference is thought to impact the placebo response (Hoge & Guthiel, 1989). This placebo response, which is responsible for 25-60% of positive outcome in clinical trials, is identified as a real physiological response similar to that produced by medication (Brown University Child and Adolescent Psychopharmacology Update, 2002). Given these factors, it appears as if facilitating a positive transference to the medications could have a physiological impact via the placebo response. While factors influencing the placebo response are not well understood, one can extrapolate from the research noted earlier that relationship factors, hope, and expectation are probably involved. These factors are enhanced when a positive transference to the social worker and/or medications exists.

Positive transference responses emanating from internal experiences of self can facilitate client's openness to psychopharmacology. For clients in whom the initiation of medications confirms their fantasy of a defective self, the medications may be fully embraced as confirmation of this belief about self (Nevins, 1990). It may validate their own experience of suffering and underscore their capacity to convey these feelings and get an empathic response. Clients may experience an increased sense of self-efficacy and empowerment as taking the medications is seen as actively mastering their illness. For individuals struggling with separation individuation issues, the medications and their self-management may provide an opportunity for them to demonstrate independence and reflect positively on their sense of self (Masi et al., 1996). The medications may be a "ticket to normality" (Conrad, 1985, p. 32) or provide an identification with somebody who took meds and did well. For clients who metaphorically understand their illness as a "chemical imbalance" the initiation of medications may be experienced as validating their definition of illness and reaffirming the psychic self as healthy. Medications may also protect the client's narcissism when they fear the illness reflects character weaknesses and the medications offer an alternative explanation (Masi et al., 1996). This experience of self and the internalized beliefs can enhance a positive transference to medications.

The therapeutic alliance can have a similar impact on the metaphor and meaning constructed around medications. When a positive therapeutic alliance exists it sets the foundation for a positive transference to the medications. The initiation of medications may reinforce this alliance, as the client feels understood and cared for by the social worker. The trust established in the relationship and the social worker's positive attitude and beliefs about the medications can also become internalized and felt by the client as valid. Similarly, the pills may become transitional objects, concrete representations of the positive affect from the social worker and a symbolic form of nurturing. Dewan (1992) notes that positive transference to medications is enhanced if the client experiences the medications as further evidence of caring and nurturing by the clinician. This "feeds their dependency needs or validates their suffering as genuine" (p. 104). Morris and Schulz (1993), in the compliance literature, underscore both the transitional nature and the symbolic caring conveyed by the pills when they identify the prescription as a symbol of the prescriber's caring and the medications are "a token" of this caring (p. 601). Similarly, this can exist with the addition of another clinician, as the triangular treatment relationship offers the client another "doctor." This configuration can increase the feeling of being helped and offer to the client an additional individual to manage separation and abandonment fears or serve as "two good parental transference figures" (Gould & Busch, 1998, p. 735).

While positive transference is usually thought of as facilitating treatment, one also needs to be aware of the potential for it to negatively impact treatment. Positive transference can become problematic if the attachment to the medications is so great it prevents necessary changes in dosage or medication, symbolically gratifies oral needs, or is used as a substitute for relationships (Hoge & Guthiel, 1989). Clients can become overly attached to the medication or a particular dosage when it takes on transferential significance.

Negative Transference

While positive transference to medications and the triangular treatment arrangement can facilitate treatment, negative responses are often overlooked and have implications for adherence to the medication regime. The literature on compliance suggests that somewhere between 30 and 50% of patients do not take their medications as prescribed (Butler et al., 1996; Conrad, 1985; & Fenton et al., 1997). Clearly, when medication response is dosage dependent this has a serious impact on outcome. Various theories have been offered for the compliance statistics (Butler et al., 1996; Conrad, 1985; Fenton et al., 1997; Morris & Schulz, 1993; Stimson, 1974). Some theories identify factors in the client's social context, belief about illness and medication, motivation to change or see noncompliance as a mechanism of self-regulation. Others associate compliance with the relationship between client and physician, communication style of the doctor, therapeutic alliance, and noncompliance as an indirect way of managing that relationship. Implicit in these theories is the existence of psychological mechanisms, conscious and unconscious, which mediate how clients take medications. Gabbard and Kay (2001) assert these psychological phenomena, particularly the negative transference, greatly impacted compliance and need attention if we are to positively impact outcome. Lurie (1991) suggests we consider potential negative transference reactions when "patients fail to improve or, in fact, develop even worse symptoms following a correct intervention" (p. 354). By this he suggests, not all medication "treatment failures" should result in a reexamination of the medications, but instead an examination of the transference toward the medication trial.

Like positive transference, the negative transference can be understood in the context of the sense of self and the therapeutic alliance. The initiation of medications can threaten the integrity of the self on multiple levels. It can threaten a positive sense of self, threaten the autonomy of the self or threaten gratification of the self. The initiation of medications can be experienced as a narcissistic injury for a client who feels it is evidence of failure or weakness (Bradley, 1990). Clients may believe it indicates they didn't try hard enough, are defective or that the social worker is disappointed in them for not getting better (Hyland, 1991). Medications can come to symbolize one's badness. Nevins (1990) asserts this can result in clients refusing medications in order to protect themselves from this damaged self-concept or discontinuing them when improved so as not to be confronted with this on a daily basis. Threats to autonomy are reflected in fears of being externally controlled (Fenton et al., 1997; Dewan, 1992) or having medications and/or the prescriber become a competitor with the self for control (Hoge & Guthiel, 1989). For the adolescent experimenting with their burgeoning independence, medications can become symbolic of dependence and thus threaten autonomy (Masi et al., 1996). Medications threaten gratification when the illness or symptoms are ego syntonic, provide secondary gain, or serve a defensive function. Nevins (1990) and Hoge and Guthiel (1989) note in clients with bipolar illness that the grandiose self and gratification seeking are threatened by treatment as it is seen as attacking the mania and promoting depression. Fenton et al. (1997) echo this in clients with schizophrenia where the psychotic symptoms support a fragile self and provide "a more positive self-image than can be provided by reality" (p. 644). Lurie (1991) further identifies that illness may become a means of gratification through identification with an ill parent and thus serves a psychic stabilizing function. No matter what threatens to unconsciously interfere with the client's stable sense of self, it may destabilize the treatment.

Treatment can be derailed by clients acting out these conflicts in the therapeutic relationship or with the medications. Medications that present a threat can metaphorically be identified as a "poison," "evil," or causing one to feel like a "robot." Client's may self-regulate their medications or refuse their medications in order to reassert autonomy (Conrad, 1985; Nevins, 1990; Fenton et al., 1997). These internal conflicts can also be projected into the therapeutic triangle. This projection process can result in interpersonal or interprofessional conflicts that disguise the true source of the conflict (Smith, 1989).

The negative transference that can result from the initiation of medications may also have deleterious effects on the therapeutic alliance. The themes emerging from the literature around the relational aspects of medication treatment have to do with power and control issues and distortions that emerge about the treating clinicians (Gould and Busch, 1998; Lurie, 1991; Rubin, 2001; Weber, 1988). The power and control issues reflect an unconscious desire to defeat one or both clinicians and thus the medications serve as a vehicle for expressing this (Lurie 1991). Because of the mechanics of pill taking, the pills can become symbolic of externally controlling objects, representing the unwanted intrusion of the prescriber, social worker or family. Some clients may attempt to control the relationship or assert their autonomy by refusing them, not taking them as prescribed, or using them in suicide attempts. In this symbolic manner the taking of medications conveys the client's approval or rejection of the relationship. This self-regulation is a means of impacting or controlling the relationship with the social worker as well as the medication.

Clients may also come to believe the initiation of medication carries meaning about their social worker. They may experience the need for medication as evidence of the social worker's incompetence (Lurie, 1991) or lack of power (Dewan, 1992). Clients may experience this new treatment arrangement as reflecting the social worker's lack of interest or desire to remain involved (Morris & Schulz, 1993) or a wish by the social worker to be rid of the client. Further the imposition of medications and a triangular treatment arrangement may cause anxiety if the client believes their social worker will terminate treatment if they respond positively to medications. These beliefs risk interfering with the client's participation in the treatment and may threaten the alliance. Again, because these feelings are induced by the medications the client may self-regulate as a means of managing their internal states.

Clinicians Within the Therapeutic Triangle

Once a medication is initiated the social worker is in a triangular treatment relationship with a prescriber. While the social worker may provide psychotherapy or other psychosocial interventions, another clinician is prescribing the medications. Each clinician is intimately involved with the client and with one another. Each brings their own expertise, psychology, theories, professional standards, values and ethics, and economic pressures. Underneath these individual aspects of the individual clinician is the professional and cultural climate of mental health practice. These factors converge in our attempt to collaboratively assist the client to manage their mental health problems. Doing this smoothly and successfully requires attention to these factors on a concrete and metaphorical level and examining their expression in our countertransferential reactions.

Each clinician brings to the triangle their own personality structure and transference and countertransference reactions. Integrated into this are the unique experiences of the personal and professional self in relation to the other clinician and the medications. What is the professional training for each clinician? Is there an integrated view of different modalities? Is there suspicion, distrust, and/or devaluation of medication? Is there appreciation for the strengths of the different disciplines? Are these the result of the biases inherent in the differing professions or do they reflect more unconscious factors relating to unresolved personal issues?

One can appreciate that differences in personality structure may draw one person to a more biologically focused profession or orientation and another to a psychosocial perspective. Bradley (1990) notes that prescribing, and the practice of medicine in general, necessitates a more authoritarian, directive, scientific, hierarchical and active stance while psychosocial interventions are more collaborative, reflective, relational and nondirective. Ellison and Smith (1989) write while the social worker "may strive to increase a patient's sense of ownership and control over his or her illness, the biologically oriented clinician often works toward a seemingly incompatible goal, that of helping the patient feel less blameworthy about bearing a disease whose basis is physical" (p. 99). There are also often gender differences between clinicians which can activate a client's and/or clinician's own unresolved gender issues (Gould & Busch, 1998). These personality and gender differences impact how clinicians interface with each other as they work collaboratively.

One of the risks in the triangular treatment relationship is that one or both clinicians will lose perspective on the biopsychosocial nature of the problem. Both clinicians must appreciate the delicate dynamics that exist between the biological, psychological and social forces. The social worker must be familiar with the basics of psychopharmacology; including uses, side effects, dosages, and drug interactions. The prescriber must understand the basic goals of the psychosocial treatment, aspects of transference and countertransference and client's social functioning. This balance, if disrupted by either clinician's countertransferential responses, can interfere with the treatment.

Examining the literature on physician countertransference, as well as the author's experience, can guide social workers in identifying their own countertransferential responses to medication and the triangular treatment relationship (Bradley, 1990; Gabbard & Kay, 2001; Goldberg, Riba, & Tasman, 1991; Gould & Busch, 1998; Hoge & Guthiel, 1989; Hyland, 1991; Lurie, 1991; Rubin, 2001; Weber, 1988; Nevins, 1990). Unconscious factors, as well as the many contextual influences noted earlier, can activate social workers' feelings toward the medication and the prescriber. These can take the form of idealization, competition, suspicion, hostility, and/or blaming. Injecting these conflicts into their relationships with the other treatment providers can negatively impact the social worker's ability to effectively collaborate. These feelings can also serve as a vehicle for enacting the client's own unconscious projections or displacing social worker-client conflicts.

They can easily become displaced onto the prescriber and the treatment providers can replay earlier parental roles (Smith, 1989).

Social worker's countertransferential idealization of the medications or the prescriber can derail treatment by focusing all attention on the medication, dosing, and side effects (Gabbard, 2000). This focus on the biology over other components of individual's lives can lead to a stilted view of the illness and treatment. Not only does the client receive the message that biology is supreme and that other factors are ancillary, but the social worker risks discounting their own professionalism, perspective, and skills (Bradley, 1990). Nevins (1990) calls this stance an "inexact interpretation" conveying the belief that all problems can be understood and treated using a biological paradigm. This idealization may function as a defensive maneuver, protecting us from the anxiety about the illness or of evaluating our own practice. It is easier to look to faulty biology to explain symptoms than to integrate the impact of the illness and/or critically reflect on the nature of our therapeutic interactions (Gabbard & Kay, 2001). It can also reflect the social worker's own sense of inadequacy, in which the idealized medications or prescriber becomes the holder of all that is absent or defective in the social worker.

Social workers and prescribers can experience competitive feelings toward one another that can distort the relationships or, if not contained, be internalized by the client. Clients sense when clinicians feel competitive with one another. Conveying an attitude that one part of the treatment is more successful or necessary than another part unconsciously devalues the other treatment. When we ascribe all the credit for progress to one or the other treatment, we are conveying a hierarchical rather than an integrative relationship between treatments. Social workers subtly convey these beliefs through questioning the need for medications or suggesting alternative interventions may be superior. These criticisms are often rationalized using professional beliefs and values.

In the context of forced collaborative treatment relationships it is not uncommon for social workers to question the competence of the prescriber (Smith, 1989). In clinic settings, social workers are often expected to share clients with other practitioners with whom they barely have a relationship. In training institutions, where residents rotate in and out, social workers can be left feeling clients are being used as guinea pigs. Clients are commonly treated psychopharmacologically by their primary care physician and social workers often question their competence in managing psychiatric medications. These scenarios can result in fertile ground for enacting a social worker's own conscious and unconscious issues. Social workers can collude with the client's negative perception of their doctor (Smith, 1989); openly question the competence of the prescriber; or advocate for the client in a condescending, hostile manner. Social workers need to contain the impulse to rescue the client or "teach" the prescriber and instead address the conflicts in a professional and collaborative manner. Otherwise, they risk undermining the psychopharmacology, the therapeutic alliance with the prescriber, as well as acting out the client's transferential material.

The client who understands their illness as a "chemical imbalance" can activate in some social workers a blaming, judgmental response (Bradley, 1990). While Lurie (1991) eloquently notes this phenomenon as a defense, it is our clinical response to the client that represents true understanding as opposed to transference acting out. Attacking the treating prescriber for being "too biological" and not appreciating the dynamic nature of the illness only serves to externalize the conflict, taking what is essentially a conflict within the client and making it an interprofessional conflict. Other countertransferential responses to the "chemical imbalance" defense are to prematurely attack this defense or collude with it. Prematurely attacking the defense is exhibited in lecturing the client, pointing out the psychosocial aspects of their illness and/or prematurely interpreting the unconsciously driven aspects of the defense. By prematurely attacking this belief, social workers miss the opportunity to understand its psychological meaning. Colluding with the defense is usually seen in focusing on the biological aspects of the illness without attempting to understand the psychological or social impacts of the illness. Alternately, the social worker may neglect all biological aspects of the illness focusing only on psychosocial issues. Colluding with the defense can result in a fragmented and less than optimal treatment.

CONCLUSION

As a result of the changes in the mental health care delivery system, the psychopharmacology triangle is the norm for most clients in mental health treatment these days. The client, the social worker, and the prescriber are in triangular treatment relationships with each other and with the medications. These relationships are impacted by beliefs about illness and treatment, historical and cultural contexts of practice, professional values and theories, and transference and countertransference reactions. Conflicts around these issues pose a threat to positive treatment outcome. These conflicts need to be consciously understood in order to minimize the negative influences and enhance the positive influences. Practical guidelines for collaboratively treating clients in a triangular treatment relationship have been published (Bentley & Walsh, 2001; Gabbard, 2000; Gould & Busch, 1998; Kelly, 1992; Meyer & Simon, 1999b; Phillips, 1997; Tasman, Riba, & Silk, 2000) and should be consulted by clinicians involved in such treatment relationships. These guidelines offer a collaborative structure and process that provides a holding environment for both clinicians and client. This structure allows for the relational space and perspective to identify and address potential conflicts and competing beliefs. The hope is that by attending to these issues within all of the different treatment relationships, social workers can diminish their destructive potential. This collaborative treatment structure values all parts of the treatment triangle and provides a consistent and predictable holding environment for all three partners. This facilitates the appreciation of the biopsychosocial nature of mental illness and treatment and fully integrates all aspects of the client, the illness, the social worker, and the prescriber.

REFERENCES

Bentley, K.J. & Walsh, J.F. (2001). *The Social Worker and Psychotropic Medications* (2nd ed.). Belmont, CA: Brooks/Cole.

Bradley, S.S. (1990). Nonphysician psychotherapist-physician pharmacotherapist: A new model of concurrent treatment. *Psychiatric Clinics of North America*, 13 (2), 307-322.

Brown University Child and Adolescent Psychopharmacology Update (2002), Common brain changes seen in placebo, antidepressant responders. 4 (6), 5-7. Retrieved July 9, 2002, from the World Wide Web, www.medscape.com/viewarticle/436009.

Butler, C., Rollnick, S. & Stott, N. (1996). The practitioner, the patient and resistance to change: Recent ideas on compliance. *Canadian Medical Association Journal*, 154 (9), 1357-1362.

Cohen, J.A. (2003). Managed care and the evolving role of the clinical social worker in mental health. *Social Work*, 48 (1), 34-43.

Conrad, P. (1985). The meaning of medications: Another look at compliance. *Social Science and Medicine*, 20 (1), 29-37.

Delacour, E. (1996) The interpersonal school and its influence on current relational theories. In J. Berzoff, L.M. Flanagan, & P. Hertz, *Inside out and outside in: Psychodynamic clinical theory and practice in contemporary multicultural contexts* (pp. 199-219). Northvale, NJ: Jason Aronson Inc.

Dewan, M.J. (1992). Adding medications to ongoing psychotherapy: Indications and pitfalls. *American Journal of Psychotherapy*, 46 (1), 102-110.

Ellison, J.M. & Smith, J.M. (1989). Intertherapist conflict in combined treatment. In J. Ellison (Ed.), *The psychotherapist's guide to pharmacotherapy* (pp. 96-115). Chicago, IL: Year Book Medical Pub.

Fenton, W.S., Blyler, C.R. & Heinssen, R.K. (1997). Determinants of medication compliance in Schizophrenia: Empirical and clinical findings. *Schizophrenia Bulletin,* 23 (4), 637-651.

Gabbard, G.O. (2000). Combining medication with psychotherapy in the treatment of personality disorders. In J. Gunderson (Ed.), *Psychotherapy of Personality Disorders* (pp. 65-94). Washington, D.C.: APA Press.

Gabbard, G.O. & Kay, J. (2001). The fate of integrated treatment: Whatever happened to the biopsychosocial psychiatrist? *American Journal of Psychiatry,* 158 (12), 1956-1963.

Gibelman, M. & Schervish, P.H. (1997). *Who we are: A second look.* Washington, D.C.: NASW Press.

Goldberg, R.S., Riba, M. & Tasman, A. (1991). Psychiatrists' attitudes toward prescribing medications for patients treated by nonmedical psychotherapists. *Hospital and Community Psychiatry,* 42 (3), 276-280.

Gould, E. & Busch, F.N. (1998). Therapeutic triangles: Some complex clinical issues. *Psychoanalytic Inquiry,* 18(5), 730-745.

Hoge, S.K. & Guthiel, T.G. (1989). Psychology of psychopharmacology. In A. Lazare (Ed.), *Outpatient Psychiatry* (2nd ed.) (pp. 690-694). Baltimore, MD: Williams & Wilkins.

Hyland, J.M. (1991). Integrating psychotherapy and pharmacotherapy. *Bulletin of the Menninger Clinic,* 55 (2), 205-215.

Kelly, K.V. (1992). Parallel treatment: Therapy with one clinician and medication with another. *Hospital and Community Psychiatry,* 43 (8), 778-780.

Klerman, G.L. (1991). Ideological conflicts in integrating pharmacotherapy and psychotherapy. In B.D. Beitman & G.L. Klerman (Eds.), *Integrating pharmacotherapy and psychotherapy.* Washington, D.C.: American Psychiatric Press.

Lambert, M.J. & Bergin, A.E. (1994) The effectiveness of psychotherapy. In A.E. Bergin & S.L. Garfield (Eds.), *Handbook of psychotherapy and behavior change* (4th ed.). New York: John Wiley & Sons.

Lurie, S.N. (1991). Psychological issues in treatment of the "chemical imbalance." *American Journal of Psychotherapy,* 45 (3), 348-358.

Manderscheid, R.W. & Sonnenschein, M.A. (Eds.). (1996). *Mental Health, United States, 1996.* Rockville, M.D. U.S. Department of Health and Human Services, Substance Abuse and Mental Health Services Administration, Center for Mental Health.

Masi, G., Marcheschi, M., & Luccherino, L. (1996). Psychotropic medication in adolescence: Psychodynamic and clinical considerations. *Adolescence,* 31 (124), 925-932.

Meyer, D.J. & Simon, R.I. (1999a). Split treatment: Clarity between psychiatrists and psychotherapists. *Psychiatric Annals,* 29 (5), 241-245.

Meyer, D.J. & Simon, R.I. (1999b). Split treatment: Clarity between psychiatrists and psychotherapists. *Psychiatric Annals,* 29 (6), 327-332.

Miller, S.D., Duncan, B.L. & Hubble, M.A. (1997) *Escape from Babel.* New York: Norton.

Morris, L.S. & Schulz, R.M. (1993). Medication compliance: The patient's perspective. *Clinical Therapeutics*, 15 (3), 593-606.

Nevins, D.B. (1990). Psychoanalytic perspectives on the use of medication for mental illness. *Bulletin of the Menninger Clinic*, 54 (3), 323-339.

Payne, M. (1997). *Modern social work theory*. Chicago, IL: Lyceum.

Phillips, K. (1997). When to consider a psychopharmacologic intervention. In R.M. Alperin & D.G. Phillips (Eds.), *The impact of managed care on the practice of psychotherapy* (pp. 57-78). New York: Bruner/Mazel.

Prochaska, J.O., Diclemente, C.C. & Norcross, J.C. (1992). In search of how people change: Applications to addictive behaviors. *American Psychologist*, 47 (9), 1102-1114.

Rubin, J. (2001). Countertransference factors on the psychology of psychopharmacology. *Journal of the American Academy of Psychoanalysis*, 29 (4), 565-573.

Sheafor, B.F. & Horejsi, C.R. (2003). *Techniques and guidelines for social work practice*. Boston, MA: Allyn & Bacon.

Smith, J. (1989). Some dimensions of transference in combined treatment. In J. Ellison (Ed.), *The psychotherapist's guide to pharmacotherapy* (pp. 79-95). Chicago, IL: Year Book Medical Pub.

Southwick, S.M. & Yehuda, R. (1993). The interaction between pharmacotherapy and psychotherapy in the treatment of posttraumatic stress disorder. *American Journal of Psychotherapy*, 47 (3), 7-13.

Stimson, G.V. (1974). Obeying doctor's orders: A view from the other side. *Social Science and Medicine*, 8, 97-104.

Tasman, A., Riba, M.B. & Silk, K.R. (2000). *The doctor-patient relationship in pharmacotherapy: Improving effectiveness*. New York: The Guilford Press.

Weber, D. (1988). Shared combined treatment: Some transference and countertransference implications in the consultation process. *Issues in Ego Psychology*, 12(2), 105-116.

The Subjective Experience
of Youth Psychotropic Treatment

Jerry Floersch

SUMMARY. The psychotropic treatment of youth is increasing dramatically. This article examines child and adolescent psychopharmacological research and argues that social work practice and research must examine the complex relationships, social and psychological, in youth pharmacologic treatment. Regarding identity formation, this article explores the developmental consequences when youth adopt an illness narrative to make sense of everyday medication treatment. A conceptual framework for mapping the socio-cultural context of youth medication management is outlined. In the conclusion, youth psychotropic treatment is connected to a perplexing 'interpretive gap,' which highlights the subjective quality of medication treatment. *[Article copies available for a fee from The Haworth Document Delivery Service: 1-800-HAWORTH. E-mail address: <docdelivery@haworthpress.com> Website: <http://www.HaworthPress.com> © 2003 by The Haworth Press, Inc. All rights reserved.]*

KEYWORDS. Child, adolescent, psychotropic treatment, illness identity, medication management

This paper was presented at the First National Internet Conference on Social Work & Psychopharmacology, February 3-24, 2003, sponsored by the Ittleson Foundation and the Virginia Commonwealth University School of Social Work in association with Psy Broadcasting Company.

[Haworth co-indexing entry note]: "The Subjective Experience of Youth Psychotropic Treatment." Floersch, Jerry. Co-published simultaneously in *Social Work in Mental Health* (The Haworth Social Work Practice Press, an imprint of The Haworth Press, Inc.) Vol. 1, No. 4, 2003, pp. 51-69; and: *Psychiatric Medication Issues for Social Workers, Counselors, and Psychologists* (ed: Kia J. Bentley) The Haworth Social Work Practice Press, an imprint of The Haworth Press, Inc., 2003, pp. 51-69. Single or multiple copies of this article are available for a fee from The Haworth Document Delivery Service [1-800-HAWORTH, 9:00 a.m. - 5:00 p.m. (EST). E-mail address: docdelivery@haworthpress.com].

Digital Object Identifier: 10.1300J200v01n04_04

INTRODUCTION

The psychotropic treatment of children and adolescents, ages 4 to 18, increased dramatically (some estimate by 3-fold) during the last decade of the twentieth century. This increase marked a new era in treatment of early onset psychiatric disorders (Gadow, 1997; Greenhill, 1998; Jensen, Bhatara, & Vitiello, 1999; Minde, 1998; Schirm, Tobi & Zito, 2001; Safer, Zito, & Fine, 1996; Zito, Safer, & dosReis, 2000; Zito, Safer, & dosReis, 2002). The central aim of this article is to review child and adolescent psychopharmacological research and argue that social work practice and research must examine the complex relationships, social and psychological, in youth pharmacologic treatment. By focusing on identity and the meaning of medication–issues that psychotropic treatment serves up to social work–practice, research, and ethical questions are examined, especially the socio-cultural context of medication management. In the conclusion, between the 'desired' and the 'actual' effects of psychotropic intervention, an "interpretive gap" is identified. This gap, it is argued, will always be present and will require some type of clinical, therapeutic, or personal interpretation. Consequently, involving youth as full partners in psychotropic treatment means listening and responding to how they make sense (i.e., interpret) of medication experience.

1990S: THE DECADE OF THE CHILD'S BRAIN?

In 1990, George Bush declared a decade of the brain. And though he meant this mandate to cover the sweep of human development and neuroscience, in retrospect it would seem that the child's brain was the target. In his extensive review of three decades of pediatric psychopharmacoepidemiology, Gadow (1997) documents a steady rise in the percentage of youth receiving medication. Safer and Krager (1988), extrapolating from Maryland data, estimate that nationwide 1.6 million school children were medicated for "hyperactive/inattentive symptoms." Zito et al. (2000) report a 65% increase (1988 to 1994) in the number of prescriptions written each year for preschool children; antidepressant use among youths 2-19 increased 2.9-fold (Zito, Safer, & dosReis, 2003; Zito & Safer, 2001). "The psychotropic medication visits of children and adolescents (younger than 18 years) increased significantly from 1.10 million in 1985 to 3.73 million visits in 1993 and 1994; as a proportion of all psychotropic medication visits, they increased from 3.4% to 8.2%, respectively" (Pincus, Tanielian, & Marcus, 1998, p. 528). Of youth, as many as 50% of all psychiatric inpatients, and as many as one-third of psychiatric outpatients are prescribed some type of antipsychotic (Findling, Schulz & Reed, 1998, p. 1207). Antipsychotic medication is often prescribed for adolescent inpatients, even in the absence of psychotic disorder (Zito, Craig, & Wanderling,1994). And for outpatients, the three most prescribed medications are psychostimulants, antidepressants, and antipsychotics (Kaplan, Simms, & Busner, 1994).

Prominent psychopharmacological researchers observe with regret that increased use has not produced important areas of new knowledge related to safety and adverse events (Findling & Dogin, 1998; Greenhill, Vitiello, & Abikoff, 2001; Jensen et al., 1999; Riddle, Kastelic, & Frosch, 2001; Vitiello, 2001; Zito & Safer 2001; Zito et al., 2003). A central concern is the uncertainty about how medication influences physical development (Greenhill et al., 2001; Jensen et al., 1999; Riddle et al., 2001; Tosyali & Greenhill, 1998; Vitiello, 1998). Some have argued that what "is specific to psychopharmacology is that the target organ, the brain, undergoes dramatic developmental changes which involve, among others, the very neurotransmitter systems upon which psychotropic drugs act" (Vitiello, 1998, p. 582). And kids are particularly vulnerable to age-dependent toxicities (Greenhill et al., 2001, p. 877). Although paucity of empirical data has made youth research and treatment complicated, it has not deterred practitioners; findings from adult research are applied to children and adolescents. Indeed, estimates are that 75% of prescriptions are off-label (Zito & Safer, 2001), that is, never tested on youth. By reminding the larger community that children are not small adults, off-label use patterns have sent many advocates, clinicians, and researchers clamoring for child-centered efficacy tests (Emslie, Walkup, & Pliszka, 1999; Riddle et al., 2001). Although youth research is made thorny by unique ethical and informed consent issues, it is argued that these difficulties should not justify blind, off-label prescribing (Ryan, Bhatara, & Perel, 1999; Tosyali & Greenhill, 1998).

The upswing in youth psychotropic treatment has led researchers to speculate that "a number of forces working in concert have spurred changes in research perspectives and clinical practices that led to this recent boom" (Riddle et al., 2001, p. 73). Increased government funding and FDA regulatory (in 1994) adjustments have contributed to expanded child research (Vitiello, 2001; Walkup, Cruz, & Kane, 1998). Noteworthy for social work is the perception that the trend is likely due to a "growing acceptance of a disease model of childhood psychopathology" (Riddle et al., 2001, p. 73; see also, Gadow [1997] and Wilens [1999]). It has been shown that illness identities among adult users of mental health services have been associated with biological explanations of depression (Karp, 1996). How might these findings relate to childhood mental illness and the possibility of the formation of youth illness identities?

CHILD AND ADOLESCENT DEVELOPMENT, IDENTITY, AND PSYCHOTROPIC TREATMENT

Research on development has understandably focused on adverse biological effects (e.g., brain, growth, weight gain, high blood pressure, and early onset of puberty). And it is doubtful that anyone would question our obligation to keep children physically safe (Vitiello, 1998). Yet, however adverse the potential biological effects, there are equally important concerns about psychological and cultural ones. "Besides keeping an open mind and being clinically vigilant, the key to successful treatment often lies in a good understanding of developmental issues and how these can affect the timing and efficacy of psychopharmacological and behavioral treatments" (Tosayali & Greenhill, 1998, p. 1031). At some point a child confronts medicine for the first time and responding to medication itself is not extraordinary; children are typically introduced to physical medicine before mental health. With physical illness, however, the scientific community has explored how youth respond to treatment and medication, especially invasive interventions (Anderson, Ho, & Brackett, 1997; Chernoff, Ireys & DeVet, 2002; Glasgow & Anderson, 1995; Gudas, Koocher, & Wypij, 1991; Horwitz, Leaf & Leventhal, 1998; Ivers-Landis & Drotar, 2000). We have not, however, studied the myriad ways youth make sense of mental health medications. Is *"take this and it will make your fever go away"* equivalent to *"take this and it will calm and slow you down?"*

For example, how do we interpret a teenager account of medication effects (desired or actual) when their developmental predisposition, separation and autonomy from parents, poses unique challenges for interpreting their resistance to parental and physician desire for medication use (Cromer & Tarnowski, 1989; Ghaziuddin, King, & Hovey, 1999; Harrop & Trower, 2001; Rappaport & Chubinsky, 2000)? Indeed, noncompliance may not at all express a need for autonomy; it may instead be the expression of a wish to avoid side effects. We cannot know how to interpret, however, unless we take seriously the myriad ways developmental issues intermingle with youth pharmacologic treatment.

For example, maturation and development make diagnosis, the first step in the psychotropic treatment process, unusually difficult (Jensen, 1998; Vitiello, 2001). As a rough measure of this ambiguity, Zito and Safer's (2001, p. 1123) chart review showed that 55% had one diagnosis, 27% had two diagnoses, and 18% had three to ten diagnoses. Thuppal, Carlson, and Sprafkin (2002) believe that developmental issues make youth unreliable informants, especially when mania symptoms are elicited. Because "some symptoms are visible to caregivers and some are not" (Thuppal et al., 2002, p. 27) the child's input is *necessary* for accurate diagnosis. Other symptoms are difficult to clarify in structured interviews and comparative developmental norms for key symptoms are not readily available. Geller, Zimerman and William (2002a) claim there are few pediatric equivalents of adult mania symptoms (e.g., like maxed out credit cards and fourth marriages). They write that "unlike manic adults, children gave concrete answers to describe their racing thoughts. Examples are: A girl pointed to the middle of her forehead and stated, 'I need a stoplight up there'" (2002a, p. 7). Indeed, Geller et al. are alone in utilizing youth specific symptoms when establishing a diagnosis, which, they argue, if routinely practiced would decrease diagnostic unreliability. The child's maturation level will also determine how concrete or abstract their symptom perceptions will be; first, it is important to assess the child's maturation and developmental status; second, to confirm their diagnosis; and third, to prescribe their medication. In sum, Geller et al. (2002a; Geller, Zimerman, & William, 2002b) demonstrate that converting adult diagnostic markers to youth assessment requires researcher and practitioner *phenomenological* interpretation of youth symptomatology and experience.

Yet, in child and adolescent mental health, as in medicine overall, the necessary first step for a prescription is a precise diagnosis. With a diagnosis it can be argued that we are treating a disorder. Absent a diagnosis, the aim may be to "control behavior, as in the use of antipsychotics to control aggression among nonpsychotic children" (see Kaplan et al., 1994). For preschoolers, in particular, Vitiello (2001) believes there is a strong tendency to treat symptoms and behavior because diagnosable pathology is rare. In short, youth prescribed psychotropic medications are not likely to be, *in the sense of a diagnosis*, 'psychotic.' In those cases where a diagnosable disorder does not exist–or even where it is ambiguous–how do youth experience the link between the prescription (e.g., antipsychotic, antidepressant, psychostimulant) and the target symptom? If a child is not given a diagnosis for psychosis, how do they make sense of the need for antipsychotic medication? Do they use illness identities to rationalize medication use? We will not have the answers to these and many related questions if we do not study youth subjective experience.

What does it mean for a child or adolescent sense of an emerging self (and identity) if in "fact new models for conceptualizing childhood psychiatric disorders as illnesses clearly facilitates the use of psychotropic medications in the pediatric population" (Walkup et al., 1998, p. 1267)? Phenomenological research has established the formation of an illness identity among adult long-term users of health services and medication (Conrad, 1985; Charmaz, 1990; Karp, 1996; Kleinman, 1988; Riessman, 1990). It is argued that illness becomes part of the self: "I am diabetic," for example. In cases of adult schizophrenia, Sue Estroff (1993) argues that becoming a 'schizophrenic' denotes a brain *and* emotional disorder; physical illness, on the other hand, marks only one aspect of our existence. Floersch (2002) argued that community support advocates joined an illness identity with a biological explanation to help facilitate hospital closure and the subsequent transfer of monies to community clinics. And although Deborah Stone (1984) effectively argues that receiving state and federal monies requires acceptance of the state's legal category of disability, the use of an illness narrative is more than a political-economic imperative. Apparently, narratives help adults meaningfully integrate illness experience (Kleinman, 1988). David Karp (1996), for example, has demonstrated that adults are active agents in making sense of medication. He concludes that "the experience of taking antidepressant medications involves a complex and emotionally charged interpretive process in which nothing less than one's view of self is at stake" (Karp, 1996, p. 102). Karp argues that the acceptance of depression as a disease ("I am depressed") is often a predictor of positive medication compliance. Would this also be true for children and adolescents?

Are illness identities forming among youth under conditions of psychotropic treatment? Clarke's (1997) qualitative study of 20 ADHD diagnosed children between the ages of 6 and 14, a singular exception in this literature and the only clear study of children's subjective experience, found that five revealed that they experienced themselves being sick in some way, either physically or mentally, because of having ADHD (Clarke, 1997, p. 76). Since we have not conducted phenomenological studies of youth, we do not know the extent to which they use illness identities to make medication treatment meaningful (as an exception, see Henker & Whalen, 1980). If, as most developmental theory suggests, identity formation is part of the work of early and late adolescence, will an illness identity serve the same interpretive function for youth as it apparently does for adults? What does it mean for an emerging 'self' to be medicated? And finally, perhaps no illness identity forms, in which case what kind of explanatory schemes do youth utilize to rationalize the need for medication?

WHY INCLUDE YOUTH SUBJECTIVE EXPERIENCE IN PRACTICE AND RESEARCH?

Research on the subjective experience of adult psychiatric disorder and medication has resulted in important findings. Phenomenological research has provided insights into the myriad ways adult symptoms are expressed (Leff & Vaughn, 1985; Jenkins, 1991; Jenkins & Karno, 1992; Jenkins, 1994; Jenkins, 1997). Culturally sensitive assessment tools depend on subjective data to create valid diagnoses (Canino, Canino, & Arroyo, 1998; Kirmayer, 1998; Jenkins, 1998, Lewis-Fernandez, 1998; Manson & Kleinman, 1998). Most important, by investigating how illness and treatment experience is shaped by the active engagement of the person, we have learned the importance of differentiating between 'the ill' self and the effects of the illness on the self (Conrad, 1990; Kleinman, 1988; Strauss, 1989).

Although practitioners and researchers are aware of the problem of subjectivity, we have little understanding of how youth interpret experiences of the doctor's office, the researcher's clinical trial, and other medication experiences. Riddle et al. (2001), for example, list the "subjective distress associated with the symptoms" (p. 76) as one among three critical components for competent assessment of youth psychopathology. Still, researchers have reported that youth are often ridiculed for taking medication and often embarrassed or self-conscious about anti-psychotic (zombie-like) side effects (Findling & Dogin, 1998; Findling et al., 1998; Rappaport & Chubinsky, 2000). Exacerbating this is the normal, self-conscious, adolescent preoccupation with body-image and related feelings. And Clarke discovered that the most common fear of school-age (ages 8-12) children on Ritalin "was the fear of possible harm to the body" (Clarke, 1997, p. 94). "Psychoanalytic theories of development underscore the normal childhood fear of body damage and harm" (Tyson & Tyson, 1990, pp. 216-217). For example, Rappaport and Chubinsky report that

> even if the clinician has reassured the parents, children are also often apprehensive about taking medication and commonly believe that this is a final proof that they are defective. Although they may not initially express these thoughts, many children will at some point call themselves crazy, bad, or stupid as an explanation for why they take medicine. Others may fear that they are brain damaged. One 10-year-old boy who had both attentional problems and depression was seen in play therapy and initially did well on medication. He then repeatedly enacted, in play, a doctor poisoning his patient. (Rappaport & Chubinsky, 2000, p. 1199)

How do we assist in understanding the fantasies and fears generated by psychotropic treatment (Shapiro, 1996)? Do we even ask?

About the nature of personal narratives in general and their importance to social science research, Ochs and Capps succinctly state that, "we come to know ourselves as we use narrative to apprehend experiences and navigate relationships with others. The inseparability of narrative and self is grounded in the phenomenological assumption that entities are given meaning through being experienced and the notion that narrative is an essential resource in the struggle to bring experiences to conscious awareness" (Ochs & Capps, 1996, p. 21). Narratives give rise, create, and build coherent and multiple understandings of our 'being' in the world. Thus, narratives have point-of-view and temporal features. And both features are relevant to youth medication research.

First, because the diagnosis of early childhood disorders is difficult, treatment of "aggression, impulsiveness, mood instability, anxiety, and sleep disturbances are the most common reasons for clinical referral and treatment. . . . However, the immediate clinical appeal to this approach is counteracted by the lack of evidence that these symptoms have the same *meaning*" [my emphasis] (Vitiello, 2001, p. 985). Because there is no plasma level test for assessing optimal psychostimulant dosage (Findling & Dogin, 1998), moreover, the need for monitoring desired effects is left to the *'interpretation'* of behaviors or illness symptoms. It is speculated that youth psychotropic narratives are dependent on how mental health providers, family, and teachers rationalize the need for medications.

Rappaport and Chubinsky also believe that

> in trying to understand specific meanings to a child, the psychia-
> trist may find that a child with a history of seizure disorder is more
> likely to see the need for medication as evidence of brain damage
> and a child with a learning disability as confirmation that he is stu-
> pid. (Rappaport & Chubinsky, 2000, p. 1199)

Second, the temporal feature of narrative complements basic development theory, which suggests that as youth apprehend past and present
experience they gain a coherent sense of 'me.' But this sense of self
changes rapidly with age; the school-age sensibility of self is not the
same as an adolescent. And the tension between a coherent and changing sense of self produces narrative activity that "seeks to bridge a self
that felt and acted in the past, a self that feels and acts in the present, and
an anticipated or hypothetical self that is projected to feel and act in
some as yet unrealized moment" (Ochs & Capps, 1996, p. 29). What is
the school-age child's past experience with psychotropics, present experience, and future anticipated experience? Clarke, for example, found
that 11 of 20 youth feared becoming dependent on medication; she also
found that their feelings of dependency increased as their positive acceptance of psychostimulants decreased (Clarke, 1997, pp. 77-80).

Investigating point-of-view and temporal features of narrative would
help us understand differences and similarities in medication experience among youth and help to establish clinical and psychosocial community-based standards, which at present seem only concerned with
prescription type and dosage amounts (Pliszka, Greenhill, & Crismon,
2000). Moreover, "longitudinal cohort studies would permit the study
of developmental changes" (Greenhill et al., 2001; Werry, McClellan,
& Chard,1991; Zito & Safer, 2001) and the myriad ways the youthful
self variously takes in the experience of *being* medicated.

THE SOCIO-CULTURAL CONTEXT:
MANAGING YOUTH PSYCHIATRIC DISORDER
AND MEDICATIONS

Development and clinical theorists (Furman, 2001) and medication
compliance researchers (Chewning & Sleath, 1996; Chewning &
Schommer, 1996; Chewning, 1997; Sleath, 1996; Sleath, Svarstad, &
Roter, 1997) concur that the more responsibility patients assume for everyday self-care and self-monitoring, the less likely they will resist
medical treatment. Brown, Borden and Wynne (1988) found that chil-

dren with higher perceived self-control have higher rates of compliance. In one psychostimulant compliance study, sixty-five percent of the children avoided taking medication (Sleator, Ullman, & Von Neumann, 1982). Clark concluded that an ADHD child's "strong desire for self-reliance is irreconcilable" to attributions linking pills to improvement (Clark, 1997, p. 97). In a study to increase compliance, Bastiaens speculates that adolescent feelings and ideas about medication should be directly examined and modified because increasing information about psychotropic treatment alone was not enough to positively influence compliance (Bastiaens, 1995). How would a practitioner modify attitudes and feelings without a simultaneous strategy to understand how youth monitor and make sense of medications? Is self-monitoring encouraged, or do parents, teachers, and doctors monitor *for* the child?

Youth experience of psychotropic medication does not occur outside of social context. Whether the *pill* or the *self* is attributed the power to produce change is largely dependent on the socio-cultural context of medication management. Even for adults, the consumption of medication is not a singular biological event. Longhofer, Floersch, and Jenkins (2003), for example, have identified five elements of an adult medication experience: (1) presenting problem or symptoms, (2) psychiatric diagnosis and prescription assessment, (3) access to or delivery of medications, (4) monitoring for compliance and effect, and (5) reporting. These elements, in turn, unfold in a grid of social relations (for a similar argument, see Cohen, 2002); and clinical trial research is usually not concerned with the community noise of in vivo medication practice (Biederman, Mick, & Bostic, 1998; Gadow, 1997; Hoagwood & Olin, 2002; Hohmann & Shear, 2002; Riddle et al., 2001; Zito & Safer, 2001). In short, *who* does *what* and *why* matters to youth under conditions of psychotropic treatment.

A grid of relations produces the boundaries for *interpretive* contexts within which biologic effects become psychologically and sociologically *meaningful* treatment experiences. For instance, because distinguishing ADHD symptoms from mania is difficult, Geller et al. (2002b) speculate that "bipolar children may be viewed by their community practitioner gatekeepers as complicated ADHD cases. And as a result, they may have been more likely to be referred to pediatric or child psychiatry sites" (p. 23). Therefore, it is in the management of medication treatments that interpretive contexts present special problems, and it is likely that the management context shapes the quality and types of narratives generated by treatment conditions. Zito et al. (2000) found disparities in prevalence data between two Medicaid school-age populations, suggesting that "the cultural values that underlie families' decisions to accept or reject medication for behavioral or mental disorders is one reason for the difference" (p. 1029).

For youth, parental involvement in medication experience is a key grid component that must be addressed in research and practice (Clarke, 1997). Parents can feel relieved "when a physician suggests medication; it validates their concerns about the serious nature of their child's problems" (Rappaport & Chubinsky, 2000, p. 1198). Those who refuse to have children medicated, moreover, may have conflict with teachers and school administrators. Firestone (1982) found that only 10% of parents informed their doctor of discontinuation. In clinical work, Erna Furman has demonstrated that parents must have the ability to first "feel with" the child in order for the child to learn self-care abilities (Furman, 2001). Thus, youth capacity for self-monitoring and self-reporting desired and actual effects of medication is likely to depend on the parent's (ongoing) investment in self-care capacity. It seems plausible that medication self-reporting is dependent on the child's ability to observe and report on–bodily, feeling, thinking, and behavioral–experiences that become tagged to medication. If the child cannot observe and monitor, then a parent or substitute does the management work *for* them.

Typically, clinical-trial psychopharmacology does not correlate findings to the social conditions influencing medication experience (Hohmann & Shear, 2002). Nor has it investigated the myriad ways each of the five elements necessarily combine in a particular social grid (i.e., children, parents, teachers, doctors, etc.) to constitute a holistic (i.e., biological, psychological, and social) and meaningful medication narrative. But we should not expect clinical trial investigations to do such work. Instead, it is the work of social science to understand how technological interventions become socially meaningful, cultural phenomena. In the grid constituting youth medication interventions, under what circumstances do participants (e.g., parents, teachers, doctors, peers) share interpretations about intervention and effects?

Understanding *youth experience* must be seen through the grid of relations that mediates the five elements of medication management (Longhofer et al., 2003). Investigating patients' social grid of medication management reveals, for those not self-monitoring, who in the grid monitors *for* them. When managers, for example, stepped forward to report *for* the patient (Floersch, 2002), was this to be coded as patient resistance to the medication regimen? Or, was the patient simply not able to self-monitor? These questions cannot be answered with methods that fail to account for the patient's subjective experience of medication. It is crucial, then, to youth research and practice that anthropological and phenomenological methods take account of the child or adolescent point of view. Children who experience medication management as controlling–or forced–may not comply with regimen requirements. Those who allow others to monitor *for* them may be resisting the regimen. If an adolescent is prescribed an antipsychotic for aggression and not for a psychotic diagnosis, does this lead to different experience and relations in the grid of management? It is speculated that youth have many participants in their grid (i.e., parents, teachers, psychiatrists, pediatricians, social workers, friends, and siblings) but how participants negotiate everyday monitoring and reporting has not been studied. And unlike adults, children are more dependent on family; thus the youth grid of medication management will likely produce a distinctive experience.

Moreover, Floersch, in *Meds, Money, and Manners* (2002), discovered that case managers utilized psychopharmacology and practical (or situated) knowledge (e.g., "has the medication kicked in," and "it clears the mind") to rationalize the need for medication. These practical understandings performed essential community work; it was not, however, a part of manager awareness. For example, managers constantly read and coded patient actions, feelings, and thoughts in order to draw conclusions about a medication's power to produce self-directed behavior. As one imagines the blood circulating chemicals to the brain, managers worked in the grid of social relations to circulate meanings about what it meant to their clients to be medicated. To a manager, the slightest change in walk, tone of voice, and daily routine could signify the efficacy of medication. Floersch concluded that manager's medication effect interpretations would not be so difficult: (1) if drugs always produced the desired effect, and (2) if patients, understood, with the same understanding of practitioners, the relationships between medication and effects (2002, p. 178). Like managers' practical medical language, it is speculated that parents and adolescents also use a practical language, while pediatricians use a medical lexicon and psychiatrists use a medical-pharmacological language to rationalize youth medication experience. If youth have many more participants in their medication grid, then meanings will likely proliferate more for youth than in adult socio-cultural contexts. What does it mean to different grid participants to have youth behavior, feeling, or thought (i.e., target symptoms) medicated? And do grid participants rationalize the aim of mental health medication with psychopharmacological or with practical knowledge?

Youth practical understandings of medication may have large influences upon outcomes. Adult research suggests that illness identities function to produce compliance, for example. For an adolescent who does not self-identify as biologically ill (with the disease of schizophrenia, for example), how do they rationalize the need for medication? Perhaps, youth compliance is dependent on who in the social grid of medication management rationalizes the need; for an adolescent, a peer may be more important than a parent, psychiatrist, or case manager.

And finally, social scientists need to study youth subjective experience and we need to map the thematic narratives they employ to make medication utilization meaningful. While on medication, are there themes of increased mastery (Clarke, 1997) or self-esteem (Frankel, Cantwell, & Myatt, 1999)? Are there themes of sickness? How about bad and good medicated feelings, and feelings of being different (stigma) from other non-medicated peers? Findling and Dogin (1998, p. 45) estimate that 30% of psychostimulant treatment fails, thus in those cases, how do youth experience a medication failure? It is unclear what narrative themes are likely to emerge, but our understandings of adult identity, illness, and management narratives are the likely sites for beginning youth research. A consequence of not studying youth medication experience is the mere adaptation of adult understandings and interpretations and this could be as problematic to the emotional, social, and cognitive development of youth as off-label prescription is to their physical health.

CONCLUSION

No matter how chemically fine-tuned psychotropic medications become through the billions that will surely be spent toward their refinement, we will always need to interpret their effects because they are first and foremost a part of lived experience. The gap between the 'desired' effect of medication and the 'actual'–clouded, of course, by unintended side effects–will never completely close. Indeed even the smallest gap requires us to make meaning of how medicines feel in the body. And only the person consuming the medication can make it a meaningful experience. Thus, in the distance between the desired and actual psychotropic effects there will always remain a phenomenological gap that cannot be bridged by the neurotransmitters that chemicals seek to affect; neurotransmitters do not have the power to assign meaning;

however, the properties of social and psychological entities do possess these emergent powers (Sayer, 2000).

Social work is proud about the professional emphasis placed on starting where the client is. This practice axiom protects the valued principle of self-determination. At the very least, self-determination means asking youth about their experience and it means making the experience of taking medication a part of any clinical encounter that involves psychotropic treatment. Self-monitoring and self-reporting in medication management are the heart of self-determination; in short, we need clinical theory and methods for assisting youth medication experience. Once a song, a color, a pet, or a smell become part of a child's inner world, we would not abruptly take these away or add new ones without carefully imagining their effects. Medications become meaningful to youth. Yet, in the practical search for the right medication and dosage, the regimen can change as often as the weather. Constant changes are not about children who cannot be helped. Rather, perhaps it is about a socio-cultural system of psychotropic treatment that displaces onto the child the uncertainty parents, practitioners, doctors, and teachers feel when they acknowledge that a medication's desired effect has not been *actualized* in the child. Once youth have tried medication, then they and others in their social grid will make "effect" interpretations (Floersch, 2002, pp. 167-174). In sum, the phenomenological reality of youth psychotropic experience–the gap between desired and actual effects–must be addressed in our research and practice. Perhaps, the decade of the child's brain is behind us and now we can only hope that research and clinical practice will catch up and begin to interpret youth psychotropic experience as part of socio-cultural (i.e., medication management) and therapeutic relationships.

REFERENCES

Anderson, B., Ho, J., Brackett, J., Finkelstein, D., & Laffel, L. (1997). Parental involvement in diabetes management tasks: Relationships to blood glucose monitoring adherence and metabolic control in young adolescents with insulin-dependent diabetes mellitus. *Journal of Pediatrics*, 130: 257-265.

Bastiaens, L. (1995). Compliance with pharmacotherapy in adolescents: Effects of patients' and parents' knowledge and attitudes toward treatment. *Journal of Child and Adolescent Psychopharmacology*, 5(1): 39-48.

Biederman, J., Mick, E., Bostic, J. Q., Prince, J., Daly, J., Wilens, T. E., Spencer, T., Garcia-Jetton, J., Russell, R., Wozniak, J., & Faraone, S. V. (1998). The naturalistic course of pharmacologic treatment of children with manic like symptoms: A systematic chart review. *Journal of Clinical Psychiatry*, 59(Nov): 628-37.

Brown, R. T., Borden, K. A., Wynne, M. E., Spunt, A. L., & Clingerman, S. R. (1988). Patterns of compliance in a treatment program for children with attention deficit disorder. *Journal of Compliance in Health Care*, 3(1): 23-39.

Canino, I., Canino, G., & Arroyo, W. (1998). Cultural considerations for childhood disorders: How much was included in DSM-IV? *Transcultural Psychiatry*, 35: 343-356.

Charmaz, K. (1990). Discovering chronic illness: Using Grounded Theory. *Social Science Medicine*, 30(11), pp. 1161-1172.

Chernoff, R. G., Ireys, H. T., DeVet, K. A., & Young, K. J. (2002). A randomized, controlled trial of a community-based support program for families of children with chronic illness: Pediatric outcomes. *Archives of Pediatric Adolescent Medicine*, 156: 533-539.

Chewning, B. (1997). Patient involvement in pharmaceutical care: A conceptual framework. *American Journal of Pharmaceutical Education*, 61(4), 394-401.

Chewning, B., & Schommer, J. C. (1996). Increasing clients' knowledge of community pharmacists' roles. *Pharmaceutical Research*, 13(9), 1299-1304.

Chewning, B., & Sleath, B. (1996). Medication decision-making and management: A client-centered model. *Social Science & Medicine*, 42(3), 389-398.

Clarke, C. H. (1997). An exploratory study of the meaning of prescription medication to children diagnosed with attention deficit hyperactivity disorder. Ph.D. dissertation, Loyola University Chicago, Department of Social Work.

Cohen, D. (2002). Research on the drug treatment of schizophrenia: A critical appraisal and implications for social work education. *Journal of Social Work Education*, 38(2): 217-239.

Conrad, P. (1990). Qualitative research on chronic illness: A commentary on method and conceptual development. *Social Science Medicine*, 30(11): 1257-1263.

Conrad, P. (1985). The meaning of medications: Another look at compliance. *Social Science Medicine*, 20: 29-37.

Cromer, B. A., & Tarnowski, K. J. (1989). Noncompliance in adolescence: A review. *Developmental Behavioral Pediatrics*, 10(4): 207-215.

Emslie, G. J., Walkup, J. T., Pliszka, S. R., & Ernst, M. (1999). Nontricyclic antidepressants: Current trends in children and adolescents. *Journal of the American Academy of Child and Adolescent Psychiatry*, 38(5): 517-528.

Estroff, Su. (1993). Identity, Disability, and Schizophrenia: The Problem of Chronicity. In S. Lindenbaum and Margaret Lock, *Knowledge, Power, & Practice*, pp. 247-286. Berkeley: University of California Press.

Findling, R. L., & Dogin, J. W. (1998). Psychopharmacology of ADHD: Children and adolescents. *Journal of Clinical Psychiatry*, 59: 42-49.

Findling, R. L., Schulz, S. C., Reed, M. D., & Blumer, J. L. (1998). The antipsychotics—A pediatric perspective. *Pediatric Clinics of North America*, 45(5): 1205-1232.

Firestone, P. (1982). Factors associated with children's adherence to stimulant medication. *American Journal of Orthopsychiatry*, 52: 447-457.

Floersch, J. (2002). *Meds, money, and manners: The case management of severe mental illness*. New York: Columbia University Press.

Frankel, F., Cantwell, D. P., Myatt, R., & Feinberg, D. T. (1999). Do stimulants improve self-esteem in children with ADHD and peer problems? *Journal of Child and Adolescent Psychopharmacology*, 9(3): 185-194.

Furman, E. (2001) *On being and having a mother*. International Universities Press.

Gadow, K. (1997). An overview of three decades of research in pediatric psychopharmacology. *Journal of Child and Adolescent Psychopharmacology*, 7(4): 219-236.

Geller, B., Zimerman, B., Williams, M., DelBello, M.P., Bolhofner, K., Craney, J. L., P., Frazier, J., Beringer, L., & Nickelsburg, M. J. (2002b). DSM-IV mania symptoms in a prepubertal and early adolescent bipolar phenotype compared to attention-deficit hyperactive and normal controls. *Journal of Child and Adolescent Psychopharmacology*, 12(1): 11-25.

Geller, B., Zimerman, B., Williams, M., DelBello, M. P., Frazier, J., & Beringer, L. (2002a). Phenomenology of prepubertal and early adolescent bipolar disorder: Examples of elated mood, grandiose behaviors, decreased need for sleep, racing thoughts, and hypersexuality. *Journal of Child and Adolescent Psychopharmacology*, 12(1): 3-9.

Ghaziuddin, N., King, C. A., Hovey, J. D., Zaccagnini, J., & Ghaziuddin, M. (1999). Medication noncompliance in adolescents with psychiatric disorders. *Human Development*, 30(2): 103-110.

Glasgow, R. E., & Anderson, B. J. (1995). Future directions for research on pediatric chronic disease management: Lessons from diabetes. *Journal of Pediatric Psychology*, 20: 389-402.

Greenhill, L. L. (1998). The use of psychotropic medication in preschoolers: Indications, safety, and efficacy. *Canadian Journal of Psychiatry-Revue Canadienne De Psychiatrie*, 43(6): 576-581.

Greenhill, L. L., Vitiello, B., Abikoff, H., Levine, J., March, J. S. , Riddle, M. A., Capasso, L., Cooper, T., Davies, M., Fisher, P., Findling, R. L., Fried, J., Labellarte, M., McCracken, J., McMahon, D. J., Robinson, J., Skrobala, A. M., Scahill L., Walkup J., & Zito J. (2001). Improving the methods for evaluating the safety of psychotropic medications in children and adolescents. *Current Therapeutic Research–Clinical and Experimental*, 62(12): 873-884.

Gudas, L. J., Koocher, G. P., & Wypij, D. (1991). Perceptions of medical compliance in children and adolescents with cystic fibrosis. *Developmental and Behavioral Pediatrics*, 12: 236-242.

Harrop, C., & Trower, P. (2001). Why does schizophrenia develop at late adolescence? *Clinical Psychology Review*, 21(2): 241-266.

Henker, B., & Whalen, C. K. (1980). The many messages of medication: Hyperactive children's perceptions and attributions. In S. Salzinger, J. Antrobus, & J. Glick (Eds), *The ecosystem of sick child*. New York: Academic Press.

Hoagwood, K., & Olin, S. S. (2002). The NIMH blueprint for change report: Research priorities in child and adolescent mental health. *The Journal of the American Academy of Child and Adolescent Psychiatry*, 41(7): 760-767.

Hohmann, A. A., & Shear, M. K. (2002). Community-based intervention research: Coping with the noise of real life in study design. *American Journal of Psychiatry*, 159(2): 201-207.

Horwitz, S. M., Leaf, P. J., & Leventhal, J. M. (1998). Identification of psychosocial problems in pediatric primary care: Do family attitudes make a difference? *Archives of Pediatrics and Adolescent Medicine*, 152: 367-371.

Ivers-Landis, C., & Drotar, D. (2000). Parental and child knowledge of the treatment regimen for childhood chronic illnesses. In D. Drotar (Ed.), *Promoting adherence to medical treatment in chronic childhood illness: Concepts, methods and interventions*, Mahwah, NJ: L. Erlbaum Assoc., pp. 259-282.

Jenkins, J. H. (1998). Diagnostic criteria for schizophrenia and related psychotic disorders: Integration and suppression of cultural evidence in DSM-IV. *Transcultural Psychiatry*, 35: 359-378.

Jenkins, J. H. (1997). Subjective experience of persistent psychiatric disorder: Schizophrenia and depression among U.S. Latinos and Euro-Americans. *British Journal of Psychiatry*, 170: 20-25.

Jenkins, J. H. (1994). The psychocultural study of emotion and mental disorder. In P. Bock (Ed.), *Handbook of psychological anthropology*. Westport, CT: Greenwood Publishers.

Jenkins, J. H., & Karno, M. (1992). The meaning of 'expressed emotion': Theoretical issues raised by cross-cultural research. *American Journal of Psychiatry*, 149: 9-21.

Jenkins, J. H. (1991). Anthropology, Expressed Emotion, and Schizophrenia. *Ethos*, 19(4): 387-431.

Jensen, P. S., Bhatara, V. S., Vitiello, B., Hoagwood, K., Feil, M., & Burke, L. B. (1999). Psychoactive medication prescribing practices for US children: Gaps between research and clinical practice. *Journal of the American Academy of Child and Adolescent Psychiatry*, 38(5): 557-565.

Jensen, P. S. (1998). Ethical and pragmatic issues in the use of psychotropic agents in young children. *Canadian Journal of Psychiatry Revue Canadienne De Psychiatrie*, 43(Aug): 585-588.

Kaplan, S. L., Simms, R. M., & Busner, J. (1994). Prescribing practices of outpatient child psychiatrists. *Journal of the American Academy of Child and Adolescent Psychiatry*, 33(1): 35-44.

Karp, D. A. (1996). *Speaking of sadness: Depression, disconnection, and the meanings of illness*. New York: Oxford University Press.

Kirmayer, L. J. (1998). Editorial: The fate of culture in DSM-IV. *Transcultural Psychiatry*, 35: 339-342.

Kleinman, A. (1988). *The illness narratives: Suffering, healing, and the human condition*. New York: Basic Books.

Leff, J., & Vaughn, C. (Eds.) (1985). *Expressed emotion in families*. New York: Guilford Press.

Lewis-Fernandez, R. (1998). A cultural critique of the DSM-IV dissociative disorders section. *Transcultural Psychiatry*, 35: 387-400.

Longhofer, J., Floersch, J., & Jenkins, J. H. (2003). The Social Grid of Community Medication Management. *American Journal of Orthopsychiatry*, 73(1): 24-34.

Manson, S., & Kleinman, A. (1998). DSM-IV, culture and mood disorders: A critical reflection on recent progress. *Transcultural Psychiatry*, 35: 377-386.

Minde, K. (1998). The use of psychotropic medication in preschoolers: Some recent developments. *Canadian Journal of Psychiatry-Revue Canadienne De Psychiatrie*, 43(6): 571-575.

Ochs, E., & Capps, L. (1996). Narrating the self. *Annual Review of Anthropology*, 25:19-43.

Pincus, H. A., Tanielian, T. L., Marcus, S. C., Olfson, M., Zarin, D. A., Thompson, J., & Zito, J. M. (1998). Prescribing trends in psychotropic medications: Primary care, psychiatry, and other medical specialities. *Journal of American Medical Association*, 279(7): 526-531.

Pliszka, S. R., Greenhill, L. L., Crismon, M. L., Sedillo, A., Carlson, C., Conners, C. K., McCracken, J. T., Swanson, J. M., Hughes, C. W., Llana, M. E., Lopez, M., Toprac, M. G., & Texas Consensus Conference, Panel On Medication Treatment of Childhood Attention-Deficit/Hyperactivity Disorder. (2000). The Texas children's medication algorithm project: Report of the Texas consensus conference panel on medication treatment of childhood attention-deficit/hyperactivity disorder. Part I. *Journal of the American Academy of Child and Adolescent Psychiatry*, 39(7): 908-919.

Rappaport, N., & Chubinsky, P. (2000). The meaning of psychotropic medications for children, adolescents, and their families. *Journal of American Academy of Child and Adolescent Psychiatry*, 39(9): 1198-1200.

Riddle, M. A., Kastelic, E. A., & Frosch, E. (2001). Pediatric psychopharmacology. *Journal of Child Psychology and Psychiatry and Allied Disciplines*, 42(Jan): 73-90.

Riessman, C.K. (1990). Strategic uses of narrative in the presentation of self and illness. *Social Science and Medicine*, 30 (11): 1195-1200.

Ryan, N. D., Bhatara, V. S., & Perel, J. M. (1999). Mood stabilizers in children and adolescents. *Journal of the American Academy of Child and Adolescent Psychiatry*, 38(5): 529-536.

Safer, D. J., & Krager, J. M. (1988). A Survey of Medication Treatment for hyperactive/inattentive students. *Journal of American Medical Association*, 260(15): 2256-2258.

Safer, D. J., Zito, J. M., & Fine. E. M. (1996). Increased methylphenidate usage for attention deficit disorder in the 1990s. *Pediatrics*, 98(6 pt. 1): 1084-1088.

Sayer, A. (2000). *Realism and Social Science*. London: Sage Publications.

Schirm, E., Tobi, H., Zito, J. M. & de Jong-van den Berg, L. T. W. (2001). Psychotropic medication in children: A study from the Netherlands. *Pediatrics*, 108(2): 30-33.

Shapiro, T. (1996). Developmental considerations in psychopharmacology: The interaction of drugs and development. In J.M. Weiner (Ed.), *Diagnosis and Psychopharmacology of childhood and adolescent disorders*, pp. 79-95. New York: John Wiley & Sons, Inc.

Sleath, B. (1996). Pharmacist-patient relationships: Authoritarian, participatory, or default? *Patient Education and Counseling*, 28, 253-263.

Sleath, B., Svarstad, B., & Roter, D. (1997). Physician vs patient initiation of psychotropic prescribing in primary care settings: A content analysis of audiotapes. *Social Science and Medicine*, 44(4), 541-548.

Sleator, E. K., Ullmann, R. K. & von Neumann, A. (1982). How do hyperactive children feel about taking stimulants and will they tell the doctor? *Clinical Pediatrics*, 21(8): 474-479.

Stone, Deborah. (1984). *The disabled state*. Philadelphia: Temple University Press.

Strauss, J. S. (1989). Subjective experiences of schizophrenia: Toward a new dynamic psychiatry–II. *Schizophrenia Bulletin*, 15(2): 179-187.

Thuppal, M., Carlson, G. A., Sprafkin, J., & Gadow, K. (2002). Correspondence between adolescent report, parent report, and teacher report of manic symptoms. *Journal of Child and Adolescent Psychopharmacology*, 12(1): 27-35.

Tosyali, M. C., & Greenhill, L. L. (1998). Child and adolescent psychopharmacology–Important developmental issues. *Pediatric Clinics of North America*, 45(5): 1021-1035.

Tyson, P., & Tyson, R. L. (1990). *Psychoanalytic theories of development: An integration*. New Haven: Yale University Press.

Vitiello, B. (2001). Psychopharmacology for young children: Clinical needs and research opportunities. *Pediatrics*, 108(Oct): 983-9.

Vitiello, B. (1998). Pediatric psychopharmacology and the interaction between drugs and the developing brain. *Canadian Journal of Psychiatry-Revue Canadienne De Psychiatrie*, 43(6): 582-584.

Walkup, J. T., Cruz, K., Kane, S., & Geller, B. (1998). The future of pediatric psychopharmacology. *Pediatric Clinics of North America*, 45(5): 1265-1278.

Werry J. S., McClellan, J. M., & Chard, L. (1991). Childhood and adolescent schizophrenic, bipolar, and schizoaffective disorders: A clinical and outcome study. *Journal American Academy of Child and Adolescent Psychiatry*, 30: 457-465.

Wilens, T. E. (1999). *Straight Talk about Psychiatric Medications for Kids*. New York: Guilford Press.

Zito, J.M. Craig, T.J., & Wanderling, J. (1994). Pharmacoepidemiology of 330 child/adolescent psychiatric patients. *Journal of Pharmacoepidemiology*, 3(1): 47-62.

Zito, J. M., & Safer, D. J. (2001). Services and prevention: Pharmacoepidemiology of antidepressant use. *Biological Psychiatry*, 49(12): 1121-1127.

Zito, J. M., Safer, D. J., dosReis, S., Gardner, J. F., Boles, M., & Lynch, F. (2000). Trends in the prescribing of psychotropic medications to preschoolers. *JAMA-Journal of the American Medical Association*, 283(8): 1025-1030.

Zito, J. M., Safer, D. J., dosReis, S., Gardner, J. F., Magder, L., Soeken, K., Boles, M., Lynch, F., & Riddle, M. A. (2003). Psychotropic practice patterns for youth. *Archives of Pediatrics & Adolescent Medicine*, 157 (1): 17-25.

Zito, J. M., Safer, D.J., dosReis, S., Gardner, J. F., Soeken, K., Boles, M., & Lynch, F. (2002). Rising prevalence of antidepressants among US youths. *Pediatrics*, 109(5): 721-727.

Medication Effect Interpretation and the Social Grid of Management

Jeffrey Longhofer
Jerry Floersch
Janis H. Jenkins

SUMMARY. This article reports on two research projects and argues that current medication management research and practice does not represent the complexity of community-based psychotropic treatment. Ethnographic findings are used to demonstrate that a social grid of management exists to negotiate medication 'effect' interpretation. Anthropological and semi-structured interview data are used to illustrate patient subjective experience of atypical antipsychotic treatment. It is argued that 'active' and 'passive' management relationships are produced by the myriad ways individuals manage the gap between the desired and actual effects of medication. It is shown that psychological and cultural 'side effects' are as common as physical 'side effects.' *[Article copies available for a fee from The Haworth Document Delivery Service: 1-800-HAWORTH. E-mail address: <docdelivery@haworthpress.com> Website:*

Research for the study of the subjective experience of atypical antipsychotics was supported by NIMH Grant MH60232 on "Culture, Schizophrenia, and Atypical Antipsychotics," Janis H. Jenkins, P.I.

This paper was presented at the First National Internet Conference on Social Work & Psychopharmacology, February 3-24, 2003, sponsored by the Ittleson Foundation and the Virginia Commonwealth University School of Social Work in association with Psy Broadcasting Company.

[Haworth co-indexing entry note]: "Medication Effect Interpretation and the Social Grid of Management." Longhofer, Jeffrey, Jerry Floersch, and Janis H. Jenkins. Co-published simultaneously in *Social Work in Mental Health* (The Haworth Social Work Practice Press, an imprint of The Haworth Press, Inc.) Vol. 1, No. 4, 2003, pp. 71-89; and: *Psychiatric Medication Issues for Social Workers, Counselors, and Psychologists* (ed: Kia J. Bentley) The Haworth Social Work Practice Press, an imprint of The Haworth Press, Inc., 2003, pp. 71-89. Single or multiple copies of this article are available for a fee from The Haworth Document Delivery Service [1-800-HAWORTH, 9:00 a.m. - 5:00 p.m. (EST). E-mail address: docdelivery@haworthpress.com].

KEYWORDS. Psychotropic treatment, medication management, compliance, qualitative methods, severe mental illness

INTRODUCTION

For many, psychotropics offer a panacea, the final scientific and technological solution to the human experience of depression, psychosis, or disabling anxiety. Yet the research on medication management points to relationships and compliance problems well beyond the scope of psychopharmacology. Some medication recipients, for example, are passive and readily defer to expert opinion and intervention, requiring the active involvement of practitioners (Ascione, 1994; Wells & Sturm, 1996). Not surprising, therefore, research has shown that for both practitioners and clients, there exists a continuum from activity to passivity (Chewning & Sleath, 1996; Chewning, 1997; Cohen & Insel, 1996; de Vries, Duggan & Tromp, 1999; Demyttenaere, 1997; Lipowski, 1997; Sleath, 1996; Sleath, Svarstad & Roter, 1997). These states, passive and active, do not refer to chemicals circulating in the blood. They implicate social positions, feelings, and interpretations of medication events and treatment experiences.

Moreover, dissemination of laboratory discoveries is increasingly recognized as the next step in pharmacotherapy research and practice. The translation of clinical-trial data for community practice raises questions about how practitioners and researchers include or exclude client beliefs and values in treatment decision-making (Chewning, 1997; Chewning & Sleath, 1996; Gournay, 1995; Hohmann & Shear, 2002; Morris & Schulz, 1992). As a result, management models have been proposed that seek active client participation (Cameron, 1996; Gerbert, Love, & Caspers, 1999; Warren & Lutz, 2000; Warren, 1999). Medication management research has shown how all participants differ significantly in levels of involvement about prescription, compliance, and symptom monitoring (Chewning & Schommer, 1996; Chewning & Sleath, 1996; Dowell, 1990; Jordan, Hardy & Coleman, 1999; Sowers & Golden, 1999). Consequently, no matter how hopeful we remain regarding the use of chemicals to relieve mental suffering, we inevitably return to human relationships. In previous work (Longhofer, Floersch & Jenkins, 2003) we identified the social grid of medication management; here, we go further to argue that the grid exists to mediate the subjective experience of psychotropic treatment.

It is argued in this article, drawing from the management literature and from our own research, that a perplexing interpretive difficulty, what will be called a drug aporia, produces the 'activity' and 'passivity' characteristic of most medication treatment relationships. The aporia is an interpretive gap produced by the distance between the hoped-for 'desired' and the perceived 'actual' effect of psychotropic treatment. Sometimes, practitioners active in the aporia, interpret effects for clients; at other times they are passive. And many factors, including gender and ethnicity, influence the subjective experience of atypical antipsychotics (Jenkins & Miller, 2002). Much of management research has been limited to compliance and decision-making in physical medicine or to management of iatrogenic problems related to chronic mental illness (Boomsma, Dassen, & Dingemans, 1999; Bennett, Done, & Hunt, 1995; Gournay, 1995; Hamera, Rhodes, & Wegner, 1994; Roter, Hall, & Merisca, 1998; Steiner & Prochazka, 1997). Others focus entirely on the narrow problem (Atkin & Ogle, 1996; Berg, Dischler, & Wagner, 1993) of compliance and pay little attention to the complex divisions of labor resulting from deinstitutionalization; indeed, this division of labor—among psychiatrists, social workers, nurses, clients, and families—remains virtually unexplored (Jordan et al., 1999; and Longhofer et al., 2003 are exceptions). There is little interest in how compliance and related behaviors emerge from the subjective experience of medication effect interpretation and how the resulting aporia, in general, is negotiated through the *social grid of medication management*. Nor is there consideration of the deliberate and self-conscious nature of patient and practitioner interpretation of medication effects. In short, patient compliance is rarely psychologically or culturally analyzed; reasons, wants, purposes, desires, and intentions, the causes of compliance, are ignored, and their unconscious dimensions inevitably elided (Keat & Urry, 1982, p. 94).

Using data from two research projects, it is argued that current medication management research and practice does not represent the complexity of psychotropic treatment. While the broader process of managing medications includes the presenting problem, prescription assessment, delivery, monitoring for compliance and effect, and reporting (see Figure 1), this essay examines the roles of the case manager, the work of case management in effect interpretation, and client subjective experience of medication. Indeed, effects are realized in the intensity and extensivity of monitoring for effects, and in the knowledge produced in day-to-day practices and interactions among the key figures: the client, case managers, pharmacists, nurses, and psychiatrists.

First, the study of community medication management and its contribution to psychopharmacologic research, the *social grid of community medication management*, is reviewed. Second, a case example from a study of atypical antipsychotic treatment is used to empirically ground the concept 'drug aporia.' Finally, in the discussion, it is argued that practitioners and clients use the grid to mediate interpretive dilemmas.

THE SOCIAL GRID OF MEDICATION MANAGEMENT

Methods

The social grid research (Longhofer et al., 2003), conducted in a community support service setting, used ethnographic methods to explore practitioner management of medication events. Narratives, culled from field notes and recordings, were used to specifically explore community monitoring for compliance and effect. Thirty-five managers were observed in weekly team and monthly clinical meetings; these, attended by team leaders, psychiatrists, nurses, and team clinical social workers, included lengthy deliberations of individual cases. Client medical records (n = 329 cases) were analyzed for the types of psychotropic medications prescribed and a synchronic analysis was conducted; during one week, medical records were examined to determine the frequency of medication type. These were studied to establish a rough measure of the intensity of interpretation in community medication management. At this particular site medications were monitored under the rubric of strengths case management, one of the most popular management models in the country (Rapp, 1998). The program offered services to approximately 400 clients. Unlike most urban community programs, this suburban location was rich in resources, evidenced by the manager's annual salary of approximately $35,000 (Floersch, 2002). All managers were required to take an in-house examination on psychotropic medications. Although the majority had bachelor's degrees, a few had post-baccalaureate training. Managers had about 5 years of experience (median) and the average caseload was fifteen (see Floersch, 2000, 2002 for a detailed discussion of methods).

FIGURE 1. The Social Grid of Medication Management

Elements of a Medication Event	Patient	Community Social Relations	
		Informal Supports (e.g., friends, family, pharmacist, employer)	Formal Supports (e.g., case manager, nurse, psychiatrist, nutritionist)
1. Presenting Problem	X	X	
2. Prescription Assessment			X
3. Delivery and Access	X		
4. Monitoring for Compliance and Effect	X	X	X
5. Reporting			X

X = Who in the medication grid does what?

Findings

Longhofer, Floersch, and Jenkins's (2003) analysis of a suburban community mental health center identified five elements of a medication management event; thus a single medication experience can be represented as a complex social division of labor. In Figure 1, the elements are represented horizontally and the social relations mediating them are represented vertically. Understanding management requires examination of who does what and why. Most research on medication management segregates one or another element; few examine the *totality* (Estroff's 1981 work on this subject is an exception). The grid represents the social relations potentially correlated with each element of a clients' medication experience and the overlapping roles and multiple sites for management. For whatever reason, those who lack the ability to self-monitor are confronted with 24 possible sites (a single site is represented as a cell in the grid) for determining *who* will do *what*. And the intensity of external (e.g., case managers, family, nurses, and psychiatrists) monitoring is determined, in part, by client capacity to act alone at each site. Power, consequently, is differentially distributed throughout the grid and depends on social policy (Cohen, McCubbin, & Guilhème, 2001), funding mechanisms, the organization of mental health services, and, of course, the client's unique life circumstances. Each service delivery setting and associated community (i.e., rural, urban, or suburban) will produce unique management of the elements. Settings dominated by medical practice, for example, will focus attention on psychiatrists and nurses. Realistically, however, case managers play a pivotal role in monitoring medications for clients (Floersch, 2002).

Research by Longhofer et al. (2003) suggests that compliance is not one-dimensional or empirically transparent; in reality, compliance, like all events in the grid, is always in complex ways psychically, culturally, and professionally mediated (see also, Cohen, 2002; Conrad, 1985; Trostle, 1988). In the following compliance illustration, a manager reports her observation of client behavior to the case management team; she draws conclusions about failed and hoped-for medication effects:

> He had put one of his mattresses outside and it got wet from the snow and rain. It was ruined. I asked him, "why didn't you tell us? We could have found a home for it [the mattress]." It didn't cross my mind what might happen next. After I left, he went to the trash bin, got the wet mattress, and put it back on his bed. It was soaking wet! He is having a difficult time keeping the place clean. I chatted with him about his personal hygiene because he is getting a little stinky. In the way he was describing his routine, I do not think he is taking a shower. He told me that he doesn't want to take a shower because of the mirror in the bathroom. He may be getting paranoid. He so *high need* and so *low functioning* at times. Well, his shot is due soon.

It was irrational to place a wet, ruined, and foul-smelling mattress on a dry bed; it was read as a sign of disorganized thinking. The manager referred to the client as "*high need*" and "*low functioning*" because he received considerable help to clean, shop, pay bills, do laundry, and get medications. For team members this client was sometimes unable to understand or "*get it*." Floersch (2002) has shown how "get it" and "high need" are examples of situated or invented language that assisted managers in explaining client behavior when medication failed to produce desired effects. In the example above, the manager reasoned that the bathroom mirror was indicative of paranoia, which prevented him from taking showers. The medication's desired effect was captured in a typical manager oral narrative, "his shot is due." Managers often condensed complex compliance observations such as these into a single medication 'effect' interpretation. Here it was hoped that with the injection the client would take showers, clean his apartment, and demonstrate clear thinking. With respect to grid participant expectations of desired effects, Lorna Rhodes has identified the cultural implication behind the metaphor "clear the mind," which was in common use among practitioners and patients in our study (Rhodes, 1984).

We found that practitioners seek desired effects and, of course, clients experience myriad actual effects. And all parties to medication treatment, aware or not, assess and monitor effects. Once in the body, crosschecking the medicine's desired effects with the actual required continued and active monitoring. Managers constantly observed changes in behavior or symptoms and reported these to others. For example, "he had an ER [emergency] med[ication] check yesterday. He was really frightened. When he hears voices, they are usually violent and aggressive. I think it was due to a decrease in his Haldol [conventional antipsychotic]. It looks like he will need both medications [Haldol and Lithobid (antimania)]" (Longhofer et al., 2003, p. 28). This example of effect interpretation–"it looks like he will need both medications," –involved reading multiple dimensions of client reality, including polypharmacy. In assessing the hoped-for desired effect, the manager used behavioral (reference to violent), emotional (reference to frightened), and cognitive (reference to hearing voices) referents to draw the conclusion that a medication change was needed. However, which medication category, antipsychotic or antimania, would produce the desired effect, less aggression and fear? This is of particular significance because it highlights the complexity of effect interpretation with polypharmacy (e.g., Floersch found in one study (2002) of 329 clients that 40 percent were prescribed three or more drugs). Behavioral, emotional, and cognitive factors combine to challenge practitioners to speculate about cause and effect across several dimensions of client experience. Was it the client's fear that caused aggression, which caused auditory hallucinations? Or, did auditory hallucinations cause fear? Moreover, what was the role of medication? The manager thought that increased fear, aggression, and auditory hallucinations were produced by a reduction in antipsychotic medication. Consequently, even under the best of consultation circumstances–which might include the presence of self-monitoring clients, the psychiatrists, managers, and family members–the above example highlights multiple dimensions of a single 'effect' interpretation.

Medication management interpretations, not always observable in the clinical or team meetings, could only be known in the ebb and flow of daily living in the community and in the occasional visits to the mental health center. Increased manic behavior, pressured speech, and exaggerated displays of anxiety made managers wonder, "are you taking meds," [compliance monitoring] or "perhaps there isn't enough in his system" [effect monitoring]. Practitioners had no conceptual tools for undertaking interpretations, nor did they see the need to do so. Even though they consistently used a situated language (i.e., "his shot is due," "has the medication kicked in," and "it clears the mind") as a substitute for pharmacological interpretations, their invented language never became a conscious part of daily work.

Moreover, in medication case management, we saw that effect interpretation often spilled over into other life domains. In the next example, managers weighed client self-initiative, self-responsibility, and self-understanding alongside medication compliance and monitoring:

> *Case Manager 1:* We need to make a decision. His apartment looks awful. Trash is everywhere and he spills coffee everywhere. I don't know if he *gets it*.
>
> *Case Manager 2:* We are using $200 a month of our flexible money to subsidize his apartment living. I don't have a problem with $100 a month. I would like to write him a letter.
>
> *Case Manager 3:* I wonder if it is time to sit down with him and talk about this. I think we could tell him we would not subsidize a substandard apartment. He is never going to pursue working a little if we do not cut him off.
>
> *Case Manager 2:* What about meds? Did he do his labs?
>
> *Case Manager 1:* I think he did, but I don't know for sure. He likes Clozaril but if he isn't going to follow the protocol, then maybe we should change it.
>
> *Case Manager 3:* Maybe we should have a team meeting at his apartment. There are so many issues. Meds, money, and housekeeping—there are at least three issues. Let's talk to him, but separate the times and the issues.

In the statement, "we need to make a decision," we see the acknowledgement that client housekeeping was below the team's standard, especially irksome because the team subsidized his rent. A quid pro quo was expected: we finance your apartment and in return we expect it to be clean enough to avoid eviction. In this instance, no effect interpretation linked medication compliance with wellness. Rather, unpredictable adherence was evidence of the client's lack of understanding ("I don't know if he gets it"). The client did not "get" that managers wanted him to see a relationship between compliance and "doing fine." In the query, "did he do his labs," managers commented on self-reliance. Intervention was considered when it was suspected that the client had not followed instructions, that is, Clozaril required weekly laboratory analysis to rule out serious side effects. Thus, when blood was not drawn for two weeks, Clozaril should be terminated. But before termination was considered, the team did *for him*–changed his medications–to prevent medication non-compliance. Here, the team feared that relapse and hospitalization would be the outcome of inadequate medication monitoring. In the above example, note in particular the complex relationship between compliance and effect interpretation: when the latter was ambiguous, the former became problematic. Was it non-compliance, failed effect, or unanticipated effect, or an even more complex dynamic among neuro-chemistry, intra and inter-psychic and social forces? The complexity was not sorted out but rather summarized in a situated, manager lexicon language: "he doesn't get it." (See Floersch, 2002).

Where self-monitoring is not possible, as in the example above, others in the grid share power or exercise it on behalf of clients, not always in helpful or caring ways. And the use of this power must be aimed at more than attempting to achieve behavioral outcomes. Throughout the life course of any specific illness, monitoring will be variably and complexly determined by a multitude of continuously changing conditions: course of illness, gender, ethnicity, social class, ability to work, family, community and cultural context, neighborhoods, quality of human relationships, emotions, social networks, type of medication, polypharmacy, and funding streams. Thus, with respect to practitioner and client management roles, we speculate that activity or passivity is dependent on (1) the level of a client's ability to self-monitor and (2) the ease of the effect interpretation. And, effect interpretation is extremely difficult when the gap between the desired and actual effect is ambiguous and open to multiple interpretations. Using client perceptions of treatment with atypical antipsychotics, we will illustrate the ambiguity present in medication effect interpretation.

CLIENT SUBJECTIVE EXPERIENCE
OF MEDICATION EFFECTS

A number of ethnographic and qualitative studies have developed methods for investigating the relationships among an illness, a person, and the person's lived experience (Csordas, 1990, 1994; Good, 1994; Karp, 1996; Kleinman, 1995; Strauss, 1994, Jenkins & Barrett, 2003). These studies include a notion of intersubjectivity alongside subjectivity, emphasizing the interactive zone of lived experience in which the self is dynamically and multiply constituted. Extending these insights into the world of medication research provides a doorway into how desired and actual effects are interpreted by the medication recipient. In research sponsored by the National Institute of Mental Health, "Culture, Schizophrenia, and Atypical Antipsychotics," Jenkins, Floersch and Longhofer are studying the subjective experience of atypical antipsychotics by incorporating the perspectives of anthropology, psychoanalysis, social work, and history.

Methods

Ninety adults (see Table 1) currently receiving outpatient treatment and management for either schizophrenia or schizo-affective illnesses (see Table 2) are included in the study. Standard research diagnostic assessments (SCID, BPRS, and SANS) have been completed on all subjects. And using the *Subjective Experience Medication Interview* (SEMI) instrument, patient experience of antipsychotic treatment and illness is examined. The SEMI tracks the multiple meanings of medication experience, which are often shifting, paradoxical, and sometimes contradictory. One focus has been the use of patient metaphors to describe medication experience. The SEMI is an open-ended anthropological interview guide designed to obtain illness and medication narratives; it queries participants about perceptions of antipsychotics. Among numerous SEMI questions and categories, those relevant for this case study are: "What do you think these medications are doing for you?"; "If you tried to explain to someone not taking this [these] medication[s] what the experience is like, what would you tell them?"; "How would you describe the effects the medication has on you?"; "What do you like about the effects of the medications?"; and, "What don't you like about the medications?"

Data analysis is currently focused on four thematic areas: (1) medication compliance, (2) emotional changes related to medication, (3) stigma linked to mental illness and medication, and (4) the usage of metaphorical language in articulating the experience of antipsychotic medication. Future analysis will investigate additional domains of gender, social relations, family life, work/employment, and experience of recovery from illness. Using a descriptive illustration, we identify the phenomenological

TABLE 1. Socio-demographic Characteristics of Participants (N =90)

	Number	Percent (%)
Gender		
Male	49	54.4
Female	41	45.6
Mean Age (s.d.)	40.7	(7.8)
Ethnicity		
European American	70	77.8
African American	20	22.2
Marital Status		
Single	74	82.2
Married/Partner	7	7.8
Divorced/Widowed/Separated	9	10.0
Living Situation		
Alone	24	26.7
Partner/Spouse	10	11.1
Relative/Parent	37	41.1
Roommate	5	5.6
Group Home	14	15.6
Have Children		
Yes	16	17.8
No	74	82.2

or interpretive gap (i.e., the medication aporia) as the paradoxical, contradictory, and ambiguous client feelings and perceptions of medication treatment.

A Case Illustration of Medication Effect Interpretation

New atypical antipsychotics have often been referred to as the "miracle drugs." Thus, each research participant was asked if their medication experience could be characterized as a miracle. In one case, the client replied:

> I don't know. I simply don't know. It's freed my anxiety level. The thing I don't know about the [medication] is that my environment has changed so many times since I've been on it. First I started taking it when I was [back east]. And then, when I came home [here] I

was living with a guy . . . And then with two guys. So as far as the effects of the medications on me, it must be so complicated because there is an interaction going on between my environment and when I take the pills. So I don't know how to judge it.

In a follow up question–"since you started taking it, do you feel different in yourself in any way?"–the same respondent, with an upbeat tone, noted:

I feel like a different person. I have self-confidence now. I dropped six pounds last week. And now I know I can do it because I play tennis and golf every Monday and Wednesday. . . . So [I] shower and shave and [get] out of the house at 8 o'clock, that's cool. . . . And now when . . . I hear words about the computer like upload and download and megabytes and modem and stuff that all [my] nephews talk about, I used to go to an anxiety state.

Continuing the interview, he was asked: "what do you want medications to do for you?" "I would want it to help with anxiety. And help me find a beautiful girlfriend." And, "what would you want a medication not to do?"

I don't want it to make me gain weight. I've had enough of that excess salivation. I don't want it to make me sleep more. I don't want to feel lethargic. And I don't want tardive dyskinesia. I don't want any of the side effects to interfere with my life.

"What does the medication do best?" the interviewer asked. "One thing I've noticed is I'm losing weight slowly, that's good." With a tone of disbelief, the interviewer followed: "Because of the medication?" "Yeah, I think so. And I feel [that] my body [is] softer now." The interviewer's skeptical tone was understandable; minutes later, in the same interview, the respondent was asked, "out of the side effects that you've talked about (i.e., weight gain, drowsiness, and drooling) what bothers you the most?" Without hesitancy, the respondent remarked: "Weight gain. I don't wear the clothes that I wore during my younger days."

Excerpts from this interview demonstrate ambiguity, contradiction, and paradox. Ambiguity is evident in the respondent's indecision about the causal powers of medication: "so I don't know how to judge it." By not

TABLE 2. Clinical Characteristics of Participants (N = 90)

	Number	Percent (%)
Diagnosis		
Schizophrenic	73	81.1
Schizo-affective	17	18.9
Mean age at onset (s.d.)	20.6 (8.2)	
Mean years ill (s.d.)	20.6 (7.3)	
Mean admissions (s.d.)	7.0 (7.0)	
Out-patient treatment*		
≤ 5 years	32	35.6
6-10 years	33	36.7
11-15 years	22	24.4
≤ 16 years	3	3.3
Current atypical antipsychotic		
Clozaril/Clozapine	51	56.7
Risperdal/Risperidone	17	18.9
Zyprexa/Olanzapine	15	16.7
Seroquel/Quetiapine	6	6.7
Melperone	1	1.1

* for length of treatment at current clinical site

separating environmental from medication effects, this left the client's causal explanation in doubt and open to myriad interpretations. Yet, by pointing to a time without medication, the interviewer found the respondent felt like a "different person" since starting the medication. Indeed, there was the sense that he felt good (i.e., "cool") about waking early to exercise. Does this contradict the earlier statement about an inability to judge? To answer this question requires exploring the gap between hoped-for and actual effects. The client's hopeful medication effect seemed fantastic in the hoped-for "beautiful girlfriend." Were the girlfriend to be actualized, we do not know if he would attribute it to medication. What we do know is that he imagines the powerful possibility of medication; therefore, he opens up a very large gap between his desired and actual medication effect. In his actual dating experience, for example, how might he have claimed that medication delivered to him the hoped-for girlfriend? Even if medication could, how would the recipient know the girlfriend had been delivered by the medication? A longing feeling, such as a "beautiful girlfriend," and "happiness," were common desires when respondents were asked, "if a medication could do anything you wanted, what would you want it to do?" Most stated very clearly, however, that medication would not make them happy. And most were fully aware that the absence of happiness was attributable to their illness; its lack produced a desire that something, perhaps a medication, could produce a miracle for them. In at least one case, the association between medication and happiness was so strong the client reported pasting smiley faces on each day of her medication box; she reported her compliance behavior improved by looking at the happy faces.

In the case example, was medication causing weight gain or loss? Interview responses suggested both. Because pharmaceutical companies have identified weight gain as a side effect, the respondent's reported weight gain and reduction, empirically real and experienced by him, had several interpretable causes. He reported exercising, which could produce weight loss, and he reported complying with a regimen known to produce weight gain. Consequently, the weight reduction remarks *did not* produce a contradiction; they were statements contrary to received opinion or belief, and contrary to what was held to be established truth–the prescribed atypical antipsychotic had not been shown to reduce weight; instead, the opposite had been established. Thus, it was not a contradiction but a paradoxical *feeling* the client was attempting to sort out. On the one hand, he wanted weight reduction and had experienced it. Yet, on the other, following medication compliance, he had experienced weight gain.

Although preliminary, this case example of paradox, ambiguity, and contradiction is likely to be experienced by many. This is so because of the interpretive gap between hoped-for and actual medication effects. The actual size of the gap is dependent on numerous variables not yet fully understood. Nevertheless, the presence of the drug aporia is evident when research methods acknowledge the paradoxical, contradictory, and ambiguous feelings that recipients (and practitioners) often experience.

DISCUSSION

A medication effect interpretation will always occur alongside at least one of the five elements of a management event; they are most prominent when compliance and effect monitoring and reporting are unfolding. It is in this way that the 'activity' or 'passivity' of actors, clients or practitioners must be calibrated to careful interpretations of the reasons, wants, purposes, desires, and intentions of actors, sometimes including unconscious ones. Thus, a patient or client-centered approach cannot be predetermined and applied mechanically to any particular setting or person; this choice should be the outcome of careful, collaborative, and highly skilled medication management, not preconditions for it. Medication, rather than producing independent behavior, the intended outcome of most pharmacotherapy models, generates instead inseparable bonds between clients and managers (Floersch, 2002). Medication often becomes the crucial link and the central most important basis for establishing and maintaining a relationship. In short, in making effect interpretations practitioners evaluate the client's capacity to live in the community.

Monitoring and reporting *for* clients occurs not because practitioners do not hope for independent compliance behavior. Rather, the drug aporia requires that management participants (inter)dependently and (inter)subjectively resolve the ever-present 'effect' interpretations. In the earlier case example of a client's subjective experience of atypical antipsychotic treatment, there was no one interpretation that could finally settle his cause/effect dilemma: Is it environment or medication that produced change? Moreover, why not wish for a medication-produced girlfriend? The hoped-for or desired effect of medication has numerous permutations depending on the client's unique circumstances and social relations. Indeed, the social relations that constitute the client's grid (Longhofer, Floersch, & Jenkins, 2003) offer evidence for the importance of relationships in any pharmacotherapy intervention; the grid relations support the participant by managing the five elements (see Figure 1) of medication management. And as long as the gap between the desired and actual effect lingers–always present–the need for 'effect' interpretations will never disappear (see Floersch [2002] for examples of case manager ongoing 'effect' interpretations).

An example of physical medicine is instructive. When one takes aspirin and hopes that the headache will subside, and it does, the gap between the desired and actual effect is minimal; although rarely is it completely dissolved, perhaps, because simultaneously the person may have learned to associate relaxing with taking aspirin. Thus, we speculate that the extent to which the gap can be reduced to a minimum, for practitioner or client, doubt will fade as to the medication's lack of effectiveness. However, as long as a perplexing difficulty or aporia over assigning meaning to our subjective experience of medication exists, the resulting ambiguity and paradox will be negotiated by relationships in the grid and associated interpretations.

For community social workers and practitioners our findings suggest that clinical interventions need to help participants (1) understand how medications become meaningful; (2) acknowledge the existence and function of the grid; and (3) place medication interpretations at the center of therapeutic work. To bracket–set at the periphery–medication effects, as if they occur independent of interpretation, requires adopting a strictly technocratic and rationalistic practice. It is as if we imagine chemicals produce subjective experience without interpretation. Perhaps it is our anxiety over not knowing–and with precision–how to 'fix' mental suffering that we imagine that psychotropic effects are transparent. The drug aporia produced by psychotropic treatment is real, multi-dimensional, and must be researched and understood. To do otherwise is to retreat into a rigid mind/body dualism. Our empirical research on medication management and the subjective experience of clients puts into question dualistic thinking.

Finally, we are left with important questions about the cultural and psychological 'side' effects of psychotropic treatment. Are they not as significant as physical ones? If not, on what empirical grounds could this be argued? Indeed, pharmaceutical companies are required to list physical side effects and psychiatrists and doctors are instructed to inform their patients about them. Why would we not also consider the cultural and psychological effects in our warnings? For example, in hoping for an effect that medication *cannot* deliver, does this not constitute a negative psychological side effect? In *not* respecting cultural difference in how people make sense of medications, is this not a negative cultural side effect? If these are 'side' effects, then why are we not including psychological and cultural warnings in our routine informed consents? We may need dualist approaches in science for research purposes, but in the lives of the medicated our findings show that separating cultural, psychological, and bodily experiences will not adequately represent the medication experience. Consequently, practitioners and researchers need to take the drug aporia as seriously as they do symptom reduction and physical side effects.

REFERENCES

Ascione, F. (1994). Medication compliance in the elderly. *Generations, 18*(2), 28-33.

Atkin, P. A., & Ogle, S. J. (1996). Issues of medication compliance and the elderly. *Adverse Drug Reaction Toxicological Reviews, 15*(2), 109-18.

Bennett, J., Done, J., & Hunt, B. (1995). Assessing the side-effects of antipsychotic drugs: A survey of community psychiatric nurse practice. *Journal of Psychiatric and Mental Health Nursing, 2*(3), 177-82.

Berg, J. S., Dischler, J., Wagner, D. J., Raia, J. J., & Palmer Shevlin, N. (1993). Medication compliance: A healthcare problem. *The Annals of Pharmacotherapy, 27*(9 Suppl), 1-24.

Boomsma, J., Dassen, T., Dingemans, C., & van den Heuvel, W. (1999). Nursing interventions in crisis-oriented and long-term psychiatric home care. *Scandinavian Journal of Caring Sciences, 13*(1), 41-8.

Cameron, C. (1996). Patient compliance: Recognition of factors involved and suggestions for promoting compliance with therapeutic regimens. *Journal of Advanced Nursing, 24,* 244-250.

Chewning, B. (1997). Patient involvement in pharmaceutical care: A conceptual framework. *American Journal of Pharmaceutical Education, 61*(4), 394-401.

Chewning, B., & Schommer, J. C. (1996). Increasing clients' knowledge of community pharmacists' roles. *Pharmaceutical Research, 13*(9), 1299-1304.

Chewning, B., & Sleath, B. (1996). Medication decision-making and management: A client-centered model. *Social Science & Medicine, 42*(3), 389-398.

Cohen, D. (2002). Research on the drug treatment of schizophrenia: A critical appraisal and implications for social work education. *Journal of Social Work Education 38*(2): 217-239.

Cohen, D., McCubbin, M., Collin, J., & Pérodeau, G. (2001). Medications as social phenomena. *Health, 5*(4), 441-469.

Cohen, J. S., & Insel, P. A. (1996). The physicians' desk reference–Problems and possible improvements. *Archives of Internal Medicine, 156*(13), 1375-1380.

Conrad, P. (1985). The meaning of medications: Another look at compliance. *Social Science and Medicine, 20*(1), 29-37.

Csordas, T. J. (1990). Embodiment as a paradigm for anthropology. *Ethos, 18,* 5-47.

Csordas, T. J. (1994). *Embodiment and experience: The existential ground of culture and self.* London: Cambridge University Press.

de Vries, C. S., Duggan, C. A., Tromp, T. F. J., & Lolkje, T. W. (1999). Changing prescribing in the light of tolerability concerns: How is this best achieved? *Drug Safety, 21*(3), 153-160.

Demyttenaere, K. (1997). Compliance during treatment with antidepressants. *Journal of Affective Disorders, 43,* 27-39.

Dowell, M. S. (1990). *People's expectations of their medications: An ethnographic study.* Ph.D. dissertation, The University of Texas at Austin.

Estroff, S. (1981). *Making it crazy: An ethnography of psychiatric clients in an American community.* Berkeley: University of California Press.

Floersch, J. (2002). Meds, money, and manners: The case management of severe mental illness. New York: Coumbia University Press.

Floersch, J. (2000). Reading the case record: The oral and written narratives of social workers. *Social Service Review, 74*(2), 169-192.

Gerbert, B., Love, C., Caspers, N., Linkins, K., & Burack, J. H. (1999). "Making all the difference in the world": How physicians can help HIV-seropositive patients become more involved in their healthcare. *AIDS Patient Care and STDs, 13*(1), 29-39.

Good, B. J. (1994). *Medicine, rationality, and experience: An anthropological perspective.* Cambridge and New York: Cambridge University Press.

Gournay, K. (1995). Mental health nurses working purposefully with people with serious and enduring mental illness–An international perspective. *International Journal of Nursing Studies, 32*(Aug), 341-52.

Hamera, E. K., Rhodes, R. M., & Wegner, M. M. (1994). Monitoring of prodromal symptoms: A method for medication management of schizophrenia. *CNS Drugs, 2*(6), 440-452.

Hohmann, A. A., & Shear, M. K. (2002). Community-based intervention research: Coping with the "noise" of real life in study design. *American Journal of Psychiatry, 159*(2): 201-207.

Jenkins, J. H., & Barrett, R. J. (2003). *The edge of experience: Schizophrenia, culture, and subjectivity. Medical Anthropology Series* Cambridge, UK: Cambridge University Press.

Jenkins, J. H., & Miller, D. (2002). A new kind of evidence for mental health services and interventions: Subjective experience of atypical antipsychotic medications. Paper presented at National Institute of Mental Health conference, "Evidenced-Based Practice," Bethesda, MD. (March).

Jordan, S., Hardy, B., & Coleman, M. (1999). Medication management: An exploratory study into the role of community mental health nurses. *Journal of Advanced Nursing, 29*(5): 1068-81.

Karp, D. (1996). *Speaking of sadness: Depression, disconnection, and the meanings of illness.* Oxford: Oxford University Press.

Keat, R., & Urry, J. (1982). *Social theory as science* (2nd ed.) London: Routledge & Kegan Paul.

Kleinman, A. (1995). *Writing at the margin: Discourse between anthropology and medicine.* Berkeley: University of California Press.

Lipowski, E. (1997). Introducing theories of patient-focused care in pharmaceutical education. *American Journal of Pharmaceutical Education, 61*, 410-414.

Longhofer, J. L., Floersch, J. E., & Jenkins, J. H. (2003). The social grid of community medication management. *American Journal of Orthopsychiatry, 73*(1): 24-34.

Morris, L. S., & Schulz, R. M. (1992). Patient compliance–An overview. *Journal of Clinical Pharmacy and Therapeutics, 17*, 283-295.

Rapp, C. (1998). *The strengths model: Case management with people suffering from severe and persistent mental illness.* New York: Oxford University Press.

Rhodes, L. (1984). This will clear your mind: The use of metaphors for medication in psychiatric settings. *Culture, Medicine, & Psychiatry, 8*:49-70.

Roter, D. L., Hall, J. A., Merisca, R., Nordstrom, B., Cretin, D., & Svarstad, B. (1998). Effectiveness of interventions to improve patient compliance–A meta-analysis. *Medical Care, 36*(8), 1138-1161.

Sleath, B. (1996). Pharmacist-patient relationships: Authoritarian, participatory, or default? *Patient Education and Counseling, 28*, 253-263.

Sleath, B., Svarstad, B., & Roter, D. (1997). Physician vs patient initiation of psychotropic prescribing in primary care settings: A content analysis of audiotapes. *Social Science and Medicine, 44*(4), 541-548.

Sowers, W., & Golden, S. (1999). Psychotropic medication management in persons with co-occurring psychiatric and substance use disorders. *Journal of Psychoactive-Drugs*, Jan-Mar; *31*(1): 59-70.

Strauss, J. S. (1994). The person with schizophrenia as a person: Approaches to the subjective and complex. *British Journal of Psychiatry, 164*(suppl. 23), 103-107.

Steiner, J. F., & Prochazka, A. V. (1997). The assessment of refill compliance using pharmacy records: Methods, validity, and applications. *Journal of Clinical Epidemiology, 50*(1), 105-116.

Trostle, J. A. (1988). Medical compliance as an ideology. *Social Science & Medicine, 27*, 1299-1308.

Warren, B. J., & Lutz, W. J. (2000). A client-oriented practice model for psychiatric mental health nursing. *Archives of Psychiatric Nursing, 14*(3), 117-126.

Warren, B. J. (1999). Cultural competence in psychiatric nursing: An interlocking paradigm approach. In N. L. Keltner, L. H. Schwecke, & C. E. Bostrom (Eds.), *Psychiatric Nursing* (pp. 199-218). Chicago: Mosby.

Wells, K. B., & Sturm, R. (1996). Informing the policy process: From efficacy to effectiveness data on pharmacotherapy. *Journal of Consulting and Clinical Psychology, 64*(4), 638-645.

Ethical Dilemmas
of Practicing Social Workers
Around Psychiatric Medication:
Results of a National Study

Joseph Walsh
Rosemary Farmer
Melissa Floyd Taylor
Kia J. Bentley

SUMMARY. It is acknowledged that social workers in mental health and other settings routinely experience client-related ethical dilemmas. Further, there is wide recognition of the potential impact of ethical dilemmas on social work practice with clients who use psychotropic medication. Little is know empirically, however, about the experiences of practitioners with these dilemmas. This article describes the results of a national survey of practicing social workers regarding the nature of ethical dilemmas they face related to their work with clients on medication issues. The results make it clear that social workers regularly confront a variety of ethical dilemmas in this type of practice. Many of these dilem-

The original version of this paper was initially presented at the First National Internet Conference on Social Work & Psychopharmacology, February 3-24, 2003, sponsored by the Ittleson Foundation and the Virginia Commonwealth University School of Social Work in association with Psy Broadcasting Company.

[Haworth co-indexing entry note]: "Ethical Dilemmas of Practicing Social Workers Around Psychiatric Medication: Results of a National Study." Walsh, Joseph et al. Co-published simultaneously in *Social Work in Mental Health* (The Haworth Social Work Practice Press, an imprint of The Haworth Press, Inc.) Vol. 1. No. 4, 2003, pp. 91-105; and: *Psychiatric Medication Issues for Social Workers, Counselors, and Psychologists* (ed: Kia J. Bentley) The Haworth Social Work Practice Press, an imprint of The Haworth Press, Inc., 2003, pp. 91-105. Single or multiple copies of this article are available for a fee from The Haworth Document Delivery Service [1-800-HAWORTH, 9:00 a.m. - 5:00 p.m. (EST). E-mail address: docdelivery@haworthpress.com].

Digital Object Identifier: 10.1300J200v01n04_06

mas are related to ambiguities around the knowledge base of practice, appropriate roles of providers, and basic personal and professional values. The authors present implications of these findings for social work practice and further research. *[Article copies available for a fee from The Haworth Document Delivery Service: 1-800-HAWORTH. E-mail address: <docdelivery@haworthpress.com> Website: <http://www.HaworthPress.com> © 2003 by The Haworth Press, Inc. All rights reserved.]*

KEYWORDS. Ethical dilemmas, social work, psychiatric medication, confidentiality

Ethical dilemmas are a regular part of daily practice for social workers in mental health and other settings (Congress, 1999). Some state licensing boards are beginning to require continuing education on ethical issues, and concerns are being raised by ethical scholars in social work about such things as managed care (Reamer, 1997) and the "the demise of confidentiality" (Davidson & Davidson, 1996). Taylor (2002) argues that social workers' abilities to deal with "professional dissonance" caused by many ethical dilemmas have implications for the future of the profession. Yet, while there is a growing recognition of the importance and impact of ethical dilemmas, little is known empirically about the experience of practitioners who face these situations. This article attempts to address these issues by describing the results of a national study of ethical dilemmas faced by practicing social workers in medication management.

Social work practitioners who carry out a range of roles and activities in helping clients obtain, learn about, think about, adhere to, and manage their psychiatric medications do so in a complex professional context. Factors that influence social work's roles in psychopharmacology include (a) ambiguities around the pharmacological knowledge base of medications, (b) differing ideas about the adequacy of research, (c) the influence of drug companies on research and marketing, (d) questions about the validity of ideas about the biological etiology of mental illness, and (e) the priority of certain professional values and ethics with clients who use psychiatric medication.

While knowledge and values are both meant to guide a general approach to practice as well as provide specific direction in situational decision-making, the reality is that ambiguities and uncertainties in these areas lead to practice dilemmas and role confusion. Key issues that seem to relate to ethical conflict with respect to social work practice and psychiatric medication include:

- The preeminence of the medical model, managed care, and the authority of physicians,
- The conundrum of the historic role of social workers to be both handmaidens to physicians and vocal advocates for clients' "best interest,"
- The sometimes tenuous balance between the short term "costs" (adverse physical and psychological effects) and "benefits" (symptom reduction) of medications,
- The lack of clear knowledge about potential long-term adverse effects of medications,
- Debates about the relative effectiveness of medical and biological interventions versus psychosocial ones,
- The lack of a full understanding of the placebo effect,
- Social and cultural pressures for people to take, or not take, psychiatric medication,
- The controversial testing and use of medications with children and adolescents,
- Differing views of self-determination, paternalism, client competence, and the desirability and ability of clients' full participation in pharmacological decision-making.

The purpose of this paper is to move from conceptual notions about *potential* ethical dilemmas to a report of data collected on *actual* ethical dilemmas experienced by social workers carrying out a range of roles and activities related to psychiatric medication management. It is an attempt to respond to the call by scholars to conduct empirical investigation into how values are operationalized in practice (e.g., Rothman, Smith, Nakashima, Patterson, & Mustin, 1996). While few in number, recent studies have documented high levels of conflict in practice. For example, Motlong (1997) found that 60% of respondents experienced conflict in their practice around self-determination. Taylor (2002) likewise noted the existence of "professional dissonance" among practicing social workers in mental health settings, defined as conflict and anxiety associated with the collision between job tasks and professional values. A full understanding of dissonance, according to Taylor, may help social workers better understand barriers to excellence in practice and prevent burnout.

In the present study social workers were asked how often they experienced a specific ethical dilemma and then to subjectively rate how bothersome the dilemma was to them. The authors' hope is that gaining an accurate and full description of ethical dilemmas in medication management might be a first step in formulating "best practices" for addressing them. This may help social workers gain confidence and competence in carrying out expanding roles and tasks in psychopharmacology (Bentley & Walsh, 2002; 2001). Results of the larger study of more general social work tasks and activities in medication management are presented elsewhere (Bentley, Walsh, & Farmer, 2003). Ethical dilemmas in this study included social workers' dealing with clients, families, and physicians, negotiating information sharing and disclosure, tolerating managed care, confronting criminal behavior, respecting culture and diversity, dealing with subtle and overt coercion, and managing their own self-doubt.

METHODOLOGY

The data reported in this paper are drawn from a larger mailed survey conducted by the authors. The data-gathering phase was completed in November 2001. Questionnaire development involved a five-month process of reviewing the literature and conducting focus groups and interviews. In order to create a survey about the roles and activities of social workers that would be rooted in the knowledge and day-to-day activities related to psychiatric medication, three focus groups involving 31 practicing social workers were held at three sites in a large mid-Atlantic city. The focus group participants worked respectively in community mental health settings, private practice, and as field instructors for BSW and MSW students in a range of other human service agencies. In addition to the focus groups, one member of the research team conducted a series of individual interviews with three local psychiatrists, one family physician, and five mental health clients. The research team processed the information gathered from the focus groups and interviews to create survey items for a questionnaire that was later piloted with fourteen local social workers. The institutional review board of the researchers' home university approved the study.

Among the major research questions for the present study were: "What specific ethical dilemmas do social workers face and how bothersome are they?" Twenty questions were generated that focused on ethical dilemmas. One of those questions gave respondents an opportunity to list "other" ethical dilemmas they experienced that had not emerged during questionnaire development. The university's Survey Evaluation and Research Lab assisted with the formatting and printing of the questionnaire booklet and managed its distribution, data collection, and data entry. Survey questionnaires were mailed to a randomly selected group of members of the National Association of Social Workers who self-identified as "clinical social worker" and marked "mental health" as their field of practice. Four thousand twenty-one (4,021) surveys were mailed with a reminder postcard mailed one week later. After bad addresses and returns were subtracted, a final total of 994 usable surveys were returned out of a possible 3,790, for a response rate of 26%. Quantitative data were analyzed using SPSS 10.0 and utilizing traditional descriptive and inferential statistics. The standard for statistical significance used was .05. Responses to the question soliciting "other" ethical dilemmas were analyzed using a two-step process described by Strauss and Corbin (1998). First, data fracturing consisted of separating the responses into data units and transcribing each response onto an index card. The second step of the analysis was conceptual coding, using a card sort process.

RESULTS

Demographics

Of the survey's 994 respondents, 69.7% (n = 640) were female and 30.3% (n = 278) were male. They ranged in age from 27 to 88 years, with a mean age of 53 years and 25.1 years of practice experience. Eighty-eight percent (88%, n = 874) had their MSW degree. Only about ten percent (9.9%, n = 98) were under age 40; 56.5% (n = 556) were between 40 and 59 years, and, 31.1% (n = 309) were between 60 and 79 years. Of the 92% (n = 914) of respondents who reported an ethnicity, a large majority were Caucasian (87.4%, n = 799). Other respondents identified themselves as Hispanic (2.3%, n = 23), African American (1.6%, n = 16), Asian/Pacific Islander (1%, n = 3), and American Indian/Alaska Native (.3%, n = 3). Two percent (2.0%, n = 18) identified themselves as "other" than the above categories.

Slightly more than half (50.8%, n = 455) of the respondents worked in urban settings. Thirty-five percent (35%, n = 319) worked in suburban areas, and 13.6% (n = 122) worked in rural settings. The types of work environments included private practice (54.7%, n = 479), community mental health centers (14.7%, n = 129), state psychiatric hospitals (3.2% n = 28), private psychiatric and general hospitals (3.0% each, n = 26 for each), social service agencies (2.9%, n = 25), state or federal mental health organizations (2.5%, n = 22), residential or group homes (2.2%, n = 19), psychosocial clubhouses or drop-in centers (.2%, n = 2), and mental health advocacy organizations (.1%, n = 1). The category of "other" was checked by 13.5% (n = 118) of respondents.

Most of the respondents provided clinical services to adults (97.8%, n = 859) and children (83.0%, n = 474). Further, 98.6% of the respondents (n = 840) indicated that at least some of their adult clients were using psychiatric medications.

The Experience of Ethical Dilemmas: Quantitative Data

Frequency. In summarizing the survey results regarding the *frequency* in which dilemmas, role conflicts, and ethical struggles were experienced by social workers, the authors collapsed the categories of "very frequently," "often," and "occasionally" into one category.

A clear finding of the study is that social workers routinely experience dilemmas, role conflicts, and ethical struggles in their work with clients who use psychotropic medications. Of the 19 survey items, two were experienced in a typical month by over 60% of the respondents. These included respecting a client's decision not to take medications when continuing symptoms were evident and perceiving that a client may be over- or under-medicated. Three other items were noted by more than 40% of the social workers. These were related to dealing with long waiting lists for medication screening appointments, deciding whether to advocate for a client or encourage the client to be a self-advocate, and responding to the possible influence of managed care on a physician's decisions about medication. Two more scale items were identified by more than 30% of the respondents. These included lacking confidence in a physician's ability to effectively prescribe medications and trying to balance encouragement and coercion of clients to take their medications. Respondents experienced dilemmas related to all of the other survey items as well, at frequencies between .6% (dispensing medication) and 29.6% (disagreeing with a physician about the need for medication).

Bothersomeness. Table 1 also presents the degree to which respondents were *bothered* by each dilemma, broken down into the categories of "quite bothersome" and "somewhat bothersome." In general, data indicate that social workers are indeed bothered by the ethical dilemmas

TABLE 1. Frequency and Bothersome Rating of Dilemmas, Role Conflicts, and Ethical Struggles in the Use of Psychiatric Medication in a Typical Month

Dilemma, Conflict, or Struggle	Very frequently, Often, or Occasionally	Percent Rating Quite Bothersome	Percent Rating Somewhat Bothersome
Respecting a client's decision not to take his medications even in the face of continuing symptoms	66.5%	19.6%	57.1%
Perceiving that a client might be overmedicated or undermedicated	61.9%	34.7%	44.2%
Being concerned with long waiting lists for medication screening appointments	48.8%	60.8%	31.9%
Deciding when to advocate for your client yourself regarding a medication-related issue or push the client to advocate for him or herself	46.8%	4.9%	28.7%
Wondering about the role of managed care and reimbursement policies in a physician's decision about medication	44.3%	58.9%	29.7%
Lacking confidence in a physician's ability to effectively prescribe medication for a client	39.2%	54.6%	34.5%
Trying to find the line between coercing a client to take medication versus merely encouraging him or her to do so	31.5%	10.5%	42.3%
Disagreeing with a physician about the client's need for medication	29.6%	20.6%	49.2%
Knowing about a client's illegal or inappropriate access to prescription medication	25.5%	55.1%	31.1%
Feeling internal or external pressure to support a physician's decision around medication with which you disagree	25.2%	31.6%	52.2%
Debating about the appropriate level of disclosure to client or family about potential side effects such as sexual dysfunction or weight gain	21.6%	9.4%	41.1%
Feeling caught in the middle between family and client with respect to self-determination and medication use	20.4%	15.5%	54.0%
Accepting when a family or client's religion or culture doesn't support the use of psychiatric medication	19.6%	16.8%	46.5%
Worrying about your own role in supporting long-term use of medication not designed for long-term use	15.2%	27.4%	51.8%
Being pressured by a family or significant others to provide them information about a client's medication	15.2%	15.8%	36.3%
Having disagreement with agency/institution's policy regarding medication	13.8%	32.2%	40.0%
Being expected to provide medication education for which you feel unprepared	12.9%	23.4%	46.0%
Assisting with an order for forced medication	4.6%	12.8%	38.5%
Actually having to step outside an agency policy to deliver or dispense medications directly to a client	0.6%	48.6%	25.7%

they encounter. In every case except one (item #4, about advocacy decisions) dilemmas were rated as either "quite" or "somewhat" bothersome by more than half of the respondents. Thirteen (13) dilemmas were rated as bothersome by more than two-thirds of the respondents. The most bothersome ethical dilemma related to long waiting lists for client appointments. Interestingly, the next two most bothersome dilemmas pertained to concerns about physicians, including the possibly negative influence of managed care policies on a physician's decisions, and a lack of confidence in the physician's competence. Concerns about personal legal culpability in knowing about a client's illegal access to medication and enforcing physician decisions with which the social worker disagrees, were also among the most bothersome.

Gender. Table 2 presents the results of a gender analysis of ethical dilemmas. Note that "quite" and "somewhat" bothersome are collapsed into one category. While the frequency with which men and women experienced dilemmas, conflicts, and ethical struggles was significantly different in only two of the 19 scenarios presented, a different picture emerged with respect to the level of bothersomeness. Gender differences were significantly different for ten of the nineteen ethical dilemmas. In all ten cases the dilemma was more bothersome to the women. The greatest differences in bothersomeness (10% or more) involved concern with long waiting lists (16.1%) and deciding when to advocate for a client regarding a medication issue (16.1%). The next largest gender differences were about feeling unprepared to provide medication information (14.8%), lacking confidence in a physician's ability to effectively prescribe medication (13.5%), and struggling with acceptance that a client or family's religion or culture does not support the use of medication (10.3%).

"Other" Dilemmas Faced by Practicing Social Workers

A content analysis of the 65 write-in responses to the question inviting participants to list "other" ethical dilemmas yielded rich information about dilemmas not explicitly listed in the printed questionnaire, although some overlap was evident. Four main categories of "other" dilemmas emerged, several of which seem specific to a particular setting or population.

Funding/Economics. These dilemmas included concerns about the cost of medication for clients without insurance, the unavailability of generic medications, and the loss of funding for psychiatric home visits for medication issues with minimally cooperative clients. Some respon-

TABLE 2. Frequency and Bothersome Rating of Dilemmas, Role Conflicts, and Ethical Struggles in the Use of Psychiatric Medication in a Typical Month: Significant Gender Differences

Dilemma, Conflict, or Struggle	Very frequently, often, or occasionally		Somewhat or Quite Bothersome	
	M	F	M	F
Perceiving that a client might be overmedicated or undermedicated			78.5%	86.3%
			p < .024	
Being concerned with long waiting lists for medication screening appointments	62.7%	67.5%	64.9%	81.0%
	p < .027		p < .000	
Deciding when to advocate for your client yourself regarding a medication-related issue or push the client to advocate for him or herself			58.2%	74.3%
			p < .000	
Wondering about the role of managed care and reimbursement policies in a physician's decision about medication			55.3%	68.1%
			p < .006	
Lacking confidence in a physician's ability to effectively prescribe medication for a client			64.0%	77.5%
			p < .020	
Debating about the appropriate level of disclosure to client or family about potential side effects such as sexual dysfunction or weight gain			82.6%	92.4%
			p < .000	
Accepting when a family or client's religion or culture doesn't support the use of psychiatric medication	42%	50.5%	85.0%	95.3%
	p < .007		p < .000	
Worrying about your own role in supporting long-term use of medication not designed for long- term use			74.1%	80.4%
			p < .041	
Being pressured by a family or significant others to provide them information about a client's medication			81.3%	87.9%
			p < .032	
Being expected to provide medication education for which you feel unprepared			42.6%	57.4%
			p < .004	

dents also voiced concerns regarding managed care pressures to put clients on medications in the first place, and questioned the practice of tying payment for outpatient therapy to concurrent medication use.

The Social Worker and the Client. Several dilemmas reported by respondents centered around the client and his or her medication use, including the social worker's getting the client to consider seeing a doctor for a medication evaluation, having the client follow the physician's prescription, and communicating with the physician. Some respondents felt they needed to insist that clients remain on medication so they could responsibly provide psychosocial therapies. There were also responses that indicated ethical struggles and role conflicts around preparing commitment papers, having the credentials to initiate seclusion/restraint procedures, and having knowledge that clients are self-adjusting to their medications. Dilemmas also arose regarding a client's family. Specific instances included parents' disagreement over a child's diagnosis and treatment, disclosing substance abuse to a family, and advising family members to seek guardianship or conservatorship of their adult children. Finally, several respondents saw inadequate clinical supervision as a significant practice dilemma in treating clients.

The Social Worker and the Physician. Ethical struggles were encountered by respondents around the perceived competence of physicians, echoing some of the dilemmas listed in the questionnaire. These included concerns that derive from being in a rural area where physician's assistants provide medical evaluations, and where primary care providers prescribe most psychiatric medication. There were also concerns about the use of pre-written prescriptions, prescription writing being connected to pharmaceutical "perks," and incompetent physicians. Respondents questioned whether 20-minute sessions were adequate to assess and monitor medication, decried a lack of follow-up evaluations for their clients, and described difficulty with emergency room physicians around drug seeking issues.

Dilemmas were reported regarding disagreement over diagnoses including the requirement to accept a physician's diagnosis and prescription (or lack of either) and needing only to report outcomes rather than suggest reevaluation of the medication regimen. Several respondents felt their expertise and input was discounted by physicians, while at the same time they were asked to take on too much responsibility for medication, including being asked by medical personnel which medication was appropriate for a client, to authorize prescription refills, or to dispense medication. Other dilemmas included the physician not communicating with the social worker in a timely manner and difficulties in handling joint interviews with a client.

The Nature of Treatment. These "other" dilemmas included concerns about the recommendation for electroconvulsive therapy, client over-reliance on medication and the resulting potential for abuse, and discussing alternatives to medication such as herbal medications, acupuncture, body work, and diet in children with ADHD. Respondents expressed that there was significant pressure *not* to educate clients about alternatives to medication. These persons have to then balance a client's right to choose with existing external pressures to medicate.

DISCUSSION

These survey respondents were mainly a Caucasian, middle-aged population of very experienced social workers. The results make it clear that they confront ethical dilemmas related to psychotropic medication use on a regular basis. As noted earlier in the paper, many of these dilemmas related to ambiguities around the knowledge base of practice, appropriate roles of providers, and basic personal and professional values.

Clients' Rights to Refuse Medication

The survey item that yielded the highest percent of conflict (67% of respondents) was "respecting a client's decision not to take medications even in the face of continuing symptoms." It appears that social workers are very conflicted about whether or not a client's right to refuse medication can or should be honored. A surprising finding in Wilk's study (1994) was that 57% of social work respondents opposed the right of involuntarily committed patients to refuse treatment with psychotropic drugs. She noted that this seems to violate the value of client self-determination and may be related to either professional paternalism or practitioners' negative experiences with psychotropic drug use. This is consistent with Abramson's (1985) finding that while most social workers agree that client self-determination is a paramount value, many of them seem willing to serve as a parent-figure in some circumstances. A later study by Abramson (1989) showed that beneficence (doing good) is often more highly valued than is client autonomy (self-determination) when these values are in conflict. Other research has also found high levels of variability in the interpretation of self-determination and its use in practice (Little, 1992; Kessel & Kane, 1980).

Published debates also reflect a range of opinions on the topic of the right to refuse medication and its relationship to self-determination. For example, Bentley (1993) and Rosenson (1993), both social workers, offer opposing positions. Bentley believes that social workers should advocate for the right of psychiatric clients to refuse medication based on legal, empirical, and ethical mandates. Rosenson, a family member, argues that social workers should be prepared to override clients' refusal of medication because respect for human dignity mandates that they help clients to access whatever treatments are needed to alleviate suffering, including medications. In another debate between a physician and a social worker (Remler & Cohen, 1992), the physician argues that clients should be restricted in their right to refuse treatment with psychotropic drugs since such behavior is due to altered brain function, and the physician is the best trained person to make such decisions. The social worker argues that clients must never be forced to undergo drug treatment against their wishes since this violates constitutional rights to freedom of speech, privacy, and protection from cruel and unusual punishment.

Survey respondents also are confronted with the dualism of self-determination versus paternalism (Reamer, 1983) reporting that 32% regularly encounter the dilemma of "trying to find the line between coercing a client to take medication versus merely encouraging him or her to do so." Abramson (1985) writes that social workers at times make use of positive therapeutic relationships to "cajole, persuade or manipulate the client" (p. 391). This occurs when social workers adopt a stance of insisting that clients take medication, or strongly urge or subtly coerce them to do so, rationalizing that it is in the best interest of the client. This dilemma, of course, is more likely to occur when the social worker believes that the medication will help to alleviate the client's symptoms.

The Social Worker's Relationship with the Prescribing Physicians

Another dilemma that yielded a high frequency among respondents (62%) was perceiving that a client may be over- or under-medicated. In addition, 39% of respondents at least occasionally lack of confidence in a physician's ability to effectively prescribe medication for a client, and 30% disagree with a physician about the client's need for medication. What is the source of these dilemmas? These issues may reflect (a) frustration among social workers that they have substantial knowledge of psychotropic drugs but do not feel they can use it, (b) a lack of confidence in their knowledge of the physiological effects of medications, (c) perceived powerlessness in the face of physician authority and presumed superior expertise, or (d) resentment of the negative feelings that some physicians harbor toward social workers who get involved in medication issues. These dilemmas are among the most bothersome for social workers because they raise the basic issue of whether or not a client is being adequately treated by the prescribing physician. While rules and procedures may be in place for outright malpractice, there is a lack of clear guidelines or professional mandate to act on more subtle doubts about a client's medical care.

Gender Differences in Ethical Dilemmas

There were a few gender differences in how often men and women experienced dilemmas, conflicts, and ethical struggles, but more differences with regard to *how bothersome* the dilemmas were. Women were more often bothered by long waiting lists for medication screening appointments and by accepting when a client or family's religion or culture does not support use of medication. These differences are difficult to explain, but may support Wilk's (1994) findings that women were more supportive of client rights than were men, presuming that greater support for rights leads to greater discomfort in cases of their abridgement. It is interesting that so many ethical dilemmas inquired about in the study (both survey items that emerged from focus groups and those added by respondents to the "other" item), seem to concern *the context of a relationship* between the client and social worker. Other authors have spoken about the important role that relationships play in the lives of most women (e.g., Kaplan, 1991) and thus the dilemmas may reflect the high value placed on the relational component in medication management. Interestingly, issues that might adversely affect these relationships (such as long waiting lists, whether to advocate for a client, accepting the client's religion/culture) are experienced as more burdensome. While there is little in the social work literature on ethics that addresses gender differences, it is argued by other authors (e.g., Gilligan, 1982) that females and males make moral decisions differently. Gilligan found that girls are more oriented to care and response ideals, while boys are more oriented to justice. Still, it cannot be assumed from this study that degree of bothersomeness correlates with the nature of responsive action when a social worker experiences an ethical dilemma.

CONCLUSION

The professional literature raises discussion about the general types of ethical problems that social workers face in their day-to-day practice, but less has been written to help social workers provide ethical practice in response to specific dilemmas. Ethical dilemmas in medication management are no different. The question is–where to go from here? Interestingly, in a study that attempts to ascertain proficiency in ethical decision-making, Wesley (2002) found that BSW faculty and students readily recognize an ethical dilemma and can identify conflicting values, but show little evidence of ethical reasoning in finding solutions. Wesley argues that social workers need to become more competent to examine competing values and develop criteria for prioritizing them. Perhaps the greatest hope is in the development of assessment frameworks to deal with ethical dilemmas (e.g., Loewenberg, Dolgoff, &

Harrington, 2000; Abramson, 1996; Manning, 1997) that help social workers engage in self-reflection and take actions that are congruent with professional values. In this way, social workers can move toward greater professional authenticity. If social workers are to fully embrace expanded roles in medication management, there must be greater dialogue about the backdrop of ethical dilemmas around psychiatric medication, including the medical model and the role of social work, the facts and fictions of psychopharmacological knowledge, and the sociopolitical aspects of prescribing. It will also mean that social workers must create greater opportunities for genuine collaboration with physicians (Bentley, Walsh, & Farmer, 2003), develop more open, trusting partnerships with clients and families, and sustain a willingness to be both self-reflective and assertive.

REFERENCES

Abramson, M. (1996). Reflections on knowing oneself ethically: Toward a working framework for social work practice. *Families in Society*, 77(4), 195-201.

Abramson, M. (1989). Autonomy vs. paternalistic beneficence: Practice strategies. *Social Casework*, 70(2), 101-105.

Abramson, M. (1985). The autonomy-paternalism dilemma in social work practice. *Social Casework*, 66(7), 387-393.

Bentley, K. J. (1993). The right of psychiatric patients to refuse medication: Where should social workers stand? *Social Work*, 38(1), 101-106.

Bentley, K. J., & Walsh, J. (2002). Social workers' roles in psychopharmacotherapy. In A. R. Roberts & G. J. Greene (Eds.), *Social workers' desk reference* (pp. 643-645). NY: Oxford University Press.

Bentley, K. J., & Walsh, J. (2001). *The social worker & psychotropic medication: Toward effective collaboration with mental health clients, families, and providers (2nd ed)*. Pacific Grove, CA: Brooks/Cole.

Bentley, K. J., Walsh, J., & Farmer, R. (2003). Roles and activities of clinical social workers with psychiatric medication: Results from a national survey. Manuscript in preparation.

Congress, E. P. (1999). *Social work values and ethics*. Pacific Grove, CA: Brooks/Cole.

Davidson, J. R., & Davidson, T. (1996). Confidentiality and managed care: Ethical and legal concerns. *Health & Social Work*, 21(3), 208-215.

Gilligan, C. (1982). *In a different voice: Psychological theory and women's development*. Cambridge, MA: Harvard University Press.

Kaplan, A. G. (1991). The "self-in-relation": Implications for depression in women. In J. Jordan, A. Kaplan, J. Miller, I. Stiver, & J. Surrey (Eds.), *Women's growth in connection: Writings from the Stone Center*. New York: The Guilford Press.

Kessel, S. D., & Kane, R. A. (1980). Self-determination dissected. *Clinical Social Work Journal*, 8(3), 161-178.

Little, M. A. (1992). Client self-determination: Current trends in social work practice. (Master's Thesis, California State University, 1992). *Master's Abstracts International*, 31(01), 0155.

Loewenberg, F. M., Dolgoff, R., & Harrington, D. (2000). *Ethical decisions for social work practice (6th ed).* Itasca, IL: F. E. Peacock.

Manning, S. S. (1997). The social worker as moral citizen: Ethics in action. *Social Work*, 42(3), 223-230.

Motlong, W. K. (1997). Clinician view of the use of influence in social work practice. *Dissertation Abstracts International*, 58(09A), 3724.

Reamer, F. G. (1997). Managing ethics under managed care. *Families in Society*, 78(1), 96-101.

Reamer, F. G. (1983). The concept of paternalism in social work. *Social Service Review* (June), 254-271.

Remler, M., & Cohen, D. (1992). Should the right of mental patients to refuse treatment with psychotropic drugs be severely curtailed? In E. Gambrill & R. Pruger (Eds.). *Controversial issues in social work*. Needham Heights, MA: Allyn & Bacon.

Rosenson, M. K. (1993). Social work and the right of psychiatric patients to refuse medication: A family advocate's response. *Social Work*, 38(1), 107-112.

Rothman, J., Smith, W., Nakashima, J., Paterson, M. A., & Mustin, J. (1996). Client self-determination and professional intervention: Striking a balance. *Social Work*, 41(4), 396-405.

Strauss, A., & Corbin, J. (1998). *Basics of qualitative research: Techniques and procedures for developing grounded theory,* 2nd ed. Thousand Oaks, CA: Sage Publications.

Taylor, M. (2002). *Professional dissonance among social workers: The collision between values and job tasks in mental health practice.* Unpublished doctoral dissertation, Virginia Commonwealth University.

Wesley, S. C. (2002). Proficiency in ethical decision-making. *Arete*, 26(1), 21-31.

Wilk, R. J. (1994). Are the rights of people with mental illness still important? *Social Work*, 39(2), 167-175.

Obtaining Informed Consent
When a Profession Labels Itself
as Providing Treatment for Mental Illness

Jill Littrell

SUMMARY. This paper examines when informed consent laws mandating explanation of the risks and benefits for proposed treatments (some talk intervention) and alternative to the proposed treatments (e.g., medications) apply to the social work profession. The reasons why an explanation of alternative treatments, including explaining medications, might be part of securing informed consent are proffered . Following this, consideration of how the task of explaining alternatives might be addressed is examined. The particular example of antidepressant medications provides a context for considering how to discuss medications as a treatment alternative. The kind of information a social worker might be obligated to possess and then impart to the client in fulfilling the task of obtaining informed consent is considered. *[Article copies available for a fee from The Haworth Document Delivery Service: 1-800-HAWORTH. E-mail address: <docdelivery@haworthpress.com> Website: <http://www.HaworthPress.com> © 2003 by The Haworth Press, Inc. All rights reserved.]*

KEYWORDS. Social work, informed consent, mental illness, psychiatric medication

---

The original version of this paper was initially presented at the First National Internet Conference on Social Work & Psychopharmacology, February 3-24, 2003, sponsored by the Ittleson Foundation and the Virginia Commonwealth University School of Social Work in association with Psy Broadcasting Company.

[Haworth co-indexing entry note]: "Obtaining Informed Consent When a Profession Labels Itself as Providing Treatment for Mental Illness." Littrell, Jill. Co-published simultaneously in *Social Work in Mental Health* (The Haworth Social Work Practice Press, an imprint of The Haworth Press, Inc.) Vol. 1, No. 4, 2003, pp. 107-122; and: *Psychiatric Medication Issues for Social Workers, Counselors, and Psychologists* (ed: Kia J. Bentley) The Haworth Social Work Practice Press, an imprint of The Haworth Press, Inc., 2003, pp. 107-122. Single or multiple copies of this article are available for a fee from The Haworth Document Delivery Service [1-800-HAWORTH, 9:00 a.m. - 5:00 p.m. (EST). E-mail address: docdelivery@haworthpress.com].

Digital Object Identifier: 10.1300J200v01n04_07

Legal scholars suggest that for those states that have informed consent laws governing medical practice these laws apply to all categories of medical providers including non-physician mental health providers (Appelbaum, Lidz, & Meisel, 1987; Lidz, Meisel, Zerubavel, Carter, Sestak, & Roth, 1984). Within the NASW code of ethics it states that "Social workers should use clear and understandable language to inform clients of the purpose of the service, risks related to the service, limits to service because of requirements of a third-party payor, relevant costs, reasonable alternatives, client's right to refuse or withdraw consent, and the time frame covered by the consent" (1.03a). While informed consent entails fully discussing the risks and benefits of all proposed treatments/interventions with clients and securing their agreement to these treatments, in some states practitioners are also required to explain the risks and benefits of alternative treatments as well as the treatment which the practitioner is intending to provide (Appelbaum et al., 1987; Lidz et al., 1984). For those professions that define themselves as treating mental illness, the imperative of discussing the availability of medications for pertinent DSM-IV (Diagnostic and Statistical Manual of the American Psychiatric Association) categories even when the practitioner is not licensed to provide access to medications seems clear.

Even when a practitioner is not recommending the medication alternative, the imperative of discussing the medications options was underscored by the Osheroff v. Chesnut Lodge case. Osheroff, a physician who had recently been divorced, sought treatment at Chesnut Lodge, a psychiatric inpatient facility noted for its psychoanalytic approach. After an extended period of treatment without positive results, Osheroff sued Chesnut Lodge for failing to offer medications as a treatment alternative to the major depression for which he met DSM criteria. Osheroff was awarded significant monetary compensation and upon appeal, the insurance company for Chesnut Lodge settled out of court. At least for the medical profession, this case set the precedent that medications should be offered as an alternative (Littrell & Ashford, 1995).

But additional questions can be asked. When social worker/mental health professionals opt to assume the job of securing informed consent, does this mean that they must present medications as the best solution for individuals with mental health diagnoses? Should social workers advocate for medication compliance, or as in most other areas of social work honoring self-determination, should the social worker merely fully explain options and then allow the client to come to an informed decision? If the social worker has information that contradicts what an

MD has told a patient, can the information be shared without the social worker risking the accusation of practicing medicine without a license?

Presently the American Psychiatric Association appears to have fully embraced medications as the panacea for mental illness. The extent to which psychiatrists have come to this perspective independently or have been strongly influenced by pharmaceutical companies remains an issue of concern. Pharmaceutical houses spend an estimated $8,000 to $13,000 per physician per year on marketing. Pharmaceutical houses subsidize trips to conferences abroad for individual physicians. They monitor the prescription writing behavior of individual physicians during the year (Critser, 1996; Torrey, 2002). In terms of the sources from which physicians draw their information, pharmaceutical houses fund much of the research on the safety and efficacy of medications conducted in this country (Angel, 2000; Breggin, 1994, pp. 172-176; Fava, 2001, 2002). Any researcher's future research career can be critically jeopardized by publishing results unfavorable to a particular drug. Recognizing the conflict, *New England Journal of Medicine* has a policy against publishing editorials by individuals with ties to pharmaceutical houses. Angel (2000), an editor for that journal, remarked that it was difficult to find a psychiatrist without such ties. Finally, Angel did succeed in locating a competent, British psychiatrist to review a major published contribution to the journal. Indeed, with regard to the very real possibility that treatment with antidepressant medications sensitizes the nervous system so that a person will exhibit a chronic depressive course, Fava (1994, p. 125) wonders about the lack of debate and discussion in the literature:

> It is indeed rare to see such issues debated: is this because of some "censorship" operated by medical journals, meeting organizers, and certain pharmaceutical manufacturers?

Moreover, Fava (1995, p. 60) elsewhere notes the lack of research examining the issue of whether antidepressants may sensitize toward a chronic course. He observes:

> Certainly researchers working along these lines are likely to encounter tremendous difficulties in performing their studies and getting them funded and published. As Klein wisely pointed out, "The industry is not interested, NIMH is not interested, and the FDA is not interested. Nobody is interested."

Others as well have recognized that research unfavorable to the drug industry simply does not get published (Gilbody & Song, 2000). Moreover, more than half of the experts hired to advise the FDA on effectiveness and safety of medications have financial ties to the industry (Cauchon, 2000).

Whether the public can rely upon the individuals who are supposed to ensure our safety can thus be questioned. Perhaps the conflict of interest precludes unquestioned reliance on package inserts and those physicians who depend on drug representatives as sources of information.

MEDICATIONS FOR MAJOR DEPRESSION

Perhaps the largest amount of confusion can be expected with regard to those DSM diagnoses that offer the largest markets, viz., major depression, generalized anxiety disorders, and attention-deficit/hyperactivity disorder (ADHD). Pharmaceutical houses now direct market to the public with TV advertisements. With regard to medications for the three diagnostic groups, researchers might be particularly reluctant to publish findings at variance with the received view. Unfortunately, even informed individuals will have difficulty presenting a coherent perspective to clients because available information is contradictory and critical gaps in information are appalling. Major depression will serve as a case in point.

What Is the Efficacy of Antidepressants?

The selective serotonin reuptake blockers (citalopram/Celexa, sertraline/Zoloft, fluoxetine/Prozac, fluvoxamine/Luvox, paroxetine/Paxil) have come to dominate the market for antidepressant drugs (Thase, Blomgren, Birkett, Apter, & Tepner, 1997). Indeed these drugs are probably better than the ones they replaced, viz., the tricyclic and heterocyclic antidepressants. The SSRIs are not associated with anticholingeric side effects such as orthostatic hypotension and dry mouth. Unlike the TCAs for which a 10-day supply was sufficient to induce lethal cardiac arrhythmias, the SSRIs have limited overdose potential (Hollon, 1996). However, the SSRIs are no more effective than the older drugs (Frank & Thase, 1999; Hollister, 1988; Thomas, 1990). They still require approximately a four-week window before a response is realized. Only two thirds of patients respond to any particular drug, with some of these (usually estimated as one third) acknowledged to be placebo responders by the medical community (Littrell, 1995; Quitkin & Stewart, 1993). Less than half of those who do respond are full responders (Keller et al., 1998; Nemeroff, 1998), i.e., only one third of the typical sample are full responders (Paykel, Ramana, Cooper, Hayhurst, Kerr, & Barocka, 1995). For some 20-30%, full remission isn't attained after two years despite medication switches (Scott, 2000; see Thase et al. 2002 for efficacy of switching medications). Prozac produces a 50% improvement in symptoms in only 38% of those who start treatment and in only 56% of those who complete a full course of improvement (Bech, Cialdella, Haugh, Birkett, Hours, & Boissel, 2000). Some symptoms (psychomotor retardation and loss of insight) are more likely to remit than depressed mood, guilt, hopelessness, impairment of work and activities, and early morning insomnia (Paykel et al., 1995).

Relapse rates while on drugs are high, with as many as 9% to 60% being reported across studies (Byrne & Rothschild, 1998; Littrell, 1995; Quitkin & Stewart, 1993). Relapse rates while on medications are particularly pronounced among those who failed to achieve full recovery (Paykel et al., 1995).

The above information can be juxtaposed with the expected outcome for major depression if one receives no treatment. Any bout of major depression is anticipated to last no more than 6 months. After 24 months, 80% of individuals have recovered without medications (Littrell, 1995; Posternak & Miller, 2001). Indeed, in the days before the availability of medications, patients suffering from depression constituted very few of the long-term residents in state hospitals (Littrell, 1995; Posternak & Miller, 2001).

The expected relapse rate of those who have suffered an episode of major depression, but have never received treatment, is hard to estimate. There was a paucity of research prior to the advent of medications. However, a review of the older literature suggests that life-time relapse rate across studies was consistently lower than half the sample in any particular study (Littrell, 1994). In an attempt to determine the optimal duration of antidepressant medication treatment, many studies have taken patients who have recovered on drug (i.e., the full responders), and then switched half the sample to placebo. The researchers have then compared relapse rates in those maintained on drug versus those switched to placebo (see Littrell, 1994, for a review and Keller et al., 1998, for recent exemplar). During the typical 6 months follow-up, relapse rates among those switched to placebo are in the 70% range, although in Keller et al. (1998) it was 50%. While these studies have been interpreted as implying the need for extended periods of treatment, others have raised the possibility that the high rate of relapse among those switched to placebo reflects drug withdrawal (Greenhouse, Stangl, Kupfer, & Prien, 1991; Littrell, 1994). Fava (1994) and Byrne and Rothschild (1998) have raised the possibility that medication, per se, may prime an individual toward a chronic course with shorter interregnums of wellness between illness episodes.

Summary and some new findings: The astute reader will recognize that the eventual rate of recovery from any episode of depression in the treated versus the untreated is about the same at two years. Eighty percent will have recovered, at some point, among both the treated and the untreated. The drugs have an edge in achieving remission more quickly (Littrell, 1994). For those achieving remission through drugs, relapse rates after drugs are discontinued are very high. The high rates of relapse, following treatment discontinuation, aren't observed for individuals who recover from an acute episode with talk therapy alone or who recover without treatment (Littrell, 1994). Several explanations have been proffered for the high rate of relapse following drug discontinuation. The high rate of relapse following drug discontinuation may be attributable to drug withdrawal or because the drugs prime the brain for chronicity (Greenhouse et al., 1991; Littrell, 1995; Fava, 1994; Byrne & Rothchild, 1998).

While the above perspective was informed largely by studies published in medical journals, a recent meta-analysis published in a psychology journal calls into question whether antidepressants have any efficacy at all beyond the placebo response (Kirsch, Moore, Scoboria, & Nicholls, 2002; Kirsch & Sapirstein, 1998). The data upon which the meta-analysis was based were supplied by the Federal Drug Administration to Kirsch et al. (2002). Of course this analysis has been disputed as well (for a full discussion from the experts, access *http://journals.apa. org/prevention/*). A large multi-site study conducted by Elkin et al. (1989) found no efficacy for drugs over talk-therapy among those whose depression was not severe, so it is possible that everyone is correct in their claims but each is speaking about a different population. While disagreement will probably continue on the basic question of whether drugs have any real efficacy, even the previously cited numbers, about which there is greater consensus, did not make a strong case for the efficacy of drugs. The difference in means between the placebo and treated groups has always been a mere two points on the Hamilton rating scale (Holon, DeRubeis, Shelton, & Weiss, 2002). Regardless of which set of particulars one accepts, even the strongest case for drug efficacy is still rather weak.

Factors Contributing to the Urgency for Quick Recovery

One of the major imperatives that is raised in conjunction with medication treatment for major depression is the possibility of a suicide attempt. The risk of suicide precipitated by depression over the lifetime is 15% (Guze & Robins, 1970). In fact, the risk of suicide for bipolar disorder greatly exceeds the risk for major depression (Rihmer, Barsi, Arato, & Demeter, 1990). Among those with major depression, risk is also relatively segregated among those who have a history of personality disorders, alcoholism, a high degree of hopelessness, and poor social support systems (Bulik, Carpenter, Kupfer, & Frank, 1990; Frank & Thase, 1999). Moreover, drugs are no better than placebo treatment on the dependent measure of the number of suicide attempts and completed suicides (Khan, Khan, Leventhal, & Brown, 2001).

Sometimes the promise of better social functioning and enhanced productivity is offered as an inducement for medication compliance. The question of whether after depressed mood remits, do the formerly depressed exhibit better social functioning has been investigated. Across studies, the answer has been inconsistent (Coryell, Scheftner, Keller, Endicott, Maser, Klerman, 1993; Kocsis, Frances, Voss, Mason, Mann, & Sweeney, 1988; Miller et al., 1998; Mintz, Mintz, Arruda, & Hwang, 1992). Perhaps whatever predisposes people to mood disorder also predisposes them, independently of mood, to deficit functioning.

What About Side Effects?

The side effects for the SSRIs include agitation, weight changes, insomnia, anorgasmia, skin rashes, diarrhea, nausea, headache, tremor, motor restlessness, cognitive dysfunction, and loss of libido (Littrell, 1995; Mirrow, 1991; Thase & Kupfer, 1996). Apathy and indifference on fluoxetine and fluvoxamine seem to be dose related (Hoehn-Saric, Lipsey, & McLeod, 1990). Consistent with the reports of apathy and indifference, SSRIs seem to blunt emotional responding (empathy, surprise, irritation) of all variety (Opbroek et al., 2002). For an individual who actually has bipolar disorder, any of the antidepressant medications can induce a manic episode and rapid cycling (Littrell, 1995). More ominous is the serotonin syndrome which entails movement problems, mental clouding, restlessness, myoclonus, shivering, tremor, hyperreflexia, an inability to control one's body temperature, coma, and seizures. Severe cases have involved disseminated intravascular coagulation, rhabdomyolysis (muscle breakdown), metabolic acidosis, renal failure, myoglobinuria, respiratory distress syndrome, and mortality. Serotonin syndrome is more likely among those receiving multiple medications (Mackay, Dunn, & Mann, 1999; Mason, Morris, & Balczak, 2000; Sternbach, 1991), a practice that has been advocated in order to attempt to further ameliorate a client's partially remitted depression. Additionally, an antidepressant combined with anti-migraine preparations, anti-emetics, or cough suppressants may be associated with increased risk (Mackay et al., 1999).

While not listed on the package insert, there is evidence that Prozac does promote tumor growth and alters immune system function (Brandes et al., 1992; Crowson & Marro, 1995; Pelligrino & Bayer, 2002; Reed & Glick, 1991). It should be noted that Prozac does not induce genetic changes as assessed on an Ames test, rather, it promotes tumor growth once a malignant cell is present (Brandes et al., 1992). In terms of other long-term effects, the SSRIs block the p450 enzyme system, the system responsible for breaking down hazardous environmental chemicals. Thus, SSRIs may be risk factors for Parkinson's and/or cancer. Thus, the long-term effects of Prozac deserve careful monitoring (Preskorn & Magnus, 1994).

Is There a Withdrawal Syndrome When Drugs Are Discontinued?

Should a client who has been taking an antidepressant ever discontinue his/her medication, he/she can expect withdrawal effects. Symptoms will include cardiac arrhythmias, chills, malaise, nausea, depression, anxiety, insomnia (Littrell, 1995). Supportive talk therapy can aid in getting over the withdrawal period (Frank, Kupfer, & Perel, 1989). Thus, social workers can play an important role should a client ever wish to discontinue antidepressant medications.

What We Don't Know About How They Work

Thanks to the advent of the SSRIs the word "serotonin" has slipped into the lexicon. While it is frequently assumed that depression results from a serotonin deficiency, in fact, there isn't much consensus in the scientific community on this issue (File, Kenny, Cheeta, 2000; Handley, 1995; Jacobs & Fornal, 1999; Stahl, 1998; Thase & Kupfer, 1996). One scenario for the efficacy of Prozac is that low levels of serotonin result in depression and that Prozac, which is known to block reuptake of serotonin, is efficacious because it increases the functional level of available serotonin. However, if this theory were true, then Prozac, which increases the time that serotonin remains in the synaptic cleft, should produce an immediate impact. In fact, it takes at least several weeks prior to achieve results (Littrell, 1995).

Maier and Watkins (1998), neuroscientists, have adduced data in support of serotonin being the neurotransmitter that mediates anxiety. These researchers offer results suggesting that increased serotonin levels increase activity in the amygdala and are required for fear conditioning to inescapable shock. This is consistent with the finding that individuals who more readily process fear and anger cues tend to have alleles (gene variants) resulting in lower density of serotonin reuptake transporters. That is, among the anxiety prone as opposed to less anxiety prone individuals, serotonin naturally remains in their synaptic cleft for a longer period of time (Hariri et al., 2002).

If Maier and Watkins are correct in their characterization of serotonin as an anxiety producer, then Prozac and other SSRIs, which are purported to have anti-anxiety effects, are probably lowering serotonin levels rather than raising them in the amygdala. This view is consistent with the Mårtensson, Nyberg, Toresson, Brodin, & Bertilsson (1989) finding that after several weeks administration SSRIs reduce cerebrospinal fluid serotonin metabolite levels (CSF 5-HIAA), although Mann (1999) argues the meaning of the latter finding is subject to interpretation. Adding to the confusion about whether SSRIs raise or lower serotonin levels, with regard to extracellular levels of serotonin in the frontal cortex, there has been observation of both increased levels and decreased levels following chronic fluoxetine (Prozac) administration (Hervas, Vilaro, Romero, Scorza, Mengod, & Artigas, 2001).

Those areas of brain innervated by serotonin which might be implicated in depression have not been identified. The median raphe and dorsal raphe (the brain's major serotonergic structures) send projections to many areas (frontal cortex, amygdala, hippocampus, etc.), sometimes innervating both excitatory neurons and inhibitory neurons in the structures to which they project. Thus, the true picture of how chronic SSRIs administration impact serotonin levels and how these serotonin levels relate to mood and behavior is not likely to be simple.

There is a literature examining the effects of having naturally low levels of serotonin as measured by metabolites in CSF. Ironically, populations with naturally low levels of serotonin are noted for impulsivity, aggressiveness, and impulsive suicidal gestures (Brown & Linnoila,

1990; Linnoila, DeJong, & Virkkunen, 1989). If serotonin levels are indeed lowered rather than raised by SSRIs, then the claims of increased suicidal ideation that have been leveled against Prozac probably deserve more study.

What About Alternatives?

In the major multi-site study evaluating antidepressant against talk therapy or a combination, no difference in efficacy between drugs versus talk therapy was found between those with mild to moderate levels of depression, although drugs achieved better results for the severely depressed (Elkin et al., 1989). Drugs are faster in achieving amelioration of symptoms (Littrell, 1995). Keller et al. (2000) recently replicated the pattern of faster recovery with drugs versus talk therapy but with a lack of difference between drugs versus talk therapy in eventual percentage improved. In the Keller et al. (2000) study, a combination of talk therapy and drugs provided superior results to either treatment alone. While talk therapy and drugs are about even with regard to number of persons eventually recovering from depression, an advantage for talk therapy over drug therapy is that following treatment discontinuation, relapse is less likely (Littrell, 1994).

Exercise as a treatment for depression has demonstrated efficacy (Babyak et al., 2000). Transcranial magnetic stimulation not only has demonstrated efficacy but there is good theoretical justification for why this treatment is efficacious (Garcia-Toro, Montes, & Talavera, 2001; George et al., 1996). Although side effects of transcranial magnetic stimulation have yet to be evaluated, exercise appears associated with many benefits (viz., cardiovascular health) beyond resolution of depression and, in those without medical conditions, exercise is safe.

WHAT INFORMATION CAN SOCIAL WORKERS IMPART?

Littrell and Ashford (1995) have evaluated the issue of whether mental health professionals can offer information to clients about medications, particularly when this information might contradict what a client has been told by a physician. In fact, this issue has arisen for the nursing profession. In a particular case, a nurse's provision of information on cancer treatments precipitated a physician's complaint to a nursing board. Although the nursing board indicated its disapproval, according to the judge, the nursing board's prior failure to offer clear guidance on the issue precluded their prerogative to sanction the nurse. Nursing boards have demurred from offering guiding rules subsequently (Littrell & Ashford, 1995). Indeed, with the advent of nurse practitioners and psychologists (in New Mexico) with prescription privileges, patients decisions regarding medical treatments are no longer limited to consultations with their physicians.

Legally, professionals can talk with clients about any matter. However, when a social worker opts to provide information to a client, this social worker assumes an awesome responsibility. The social worker should provide thorough, accurate information that can be documented with valid references.

If social workers elect to discuss medications with clients, rather than referring the task of satisfying informed consent requirements to others, what ethical responsibilities do they have for preparing thorough literature searches and investigating sources of information beyond what the drug companies provide? It should be noted that the advertisements provided by drug companies are often misleading and scientifically inaccurate (Fava, 1998; Wilkes, Doblin, & Shapiro, 1992). If social workers just provide package insert information and rely only on researchers who are known consultants for the industry, then won't they be just another sales force misinforming consumers?

Usually knowledge about side effects dribbles in after a drug has been on the market for some time. This is an inevitable consequence of the way in which drugs are evaluated in this country prior to being approved by the FDA. In fact, drugs are evaluated for safety on the basis of individuals who have been receiving the drugs for a relatively short time (four-year period or less) (Alliance Pharmaceutical Corporation, 2002). When drugs go on the market, no one knows about their long-term effects. Is it ethical for anyone to provide reassurance when this reassurance is false? Presently, drug trials for antidepressant use in pregnant women and in children are being conducted. These are populations for whom the drug companies have, in the case of particular antidepressants for children, only recently assumed product liability. Can anyone ethically provide reassurance in these areas?

Perhaps, NASW needs to expand the code of ethics to include discussion of whether a social worker can be reassuring, when, in fact, no one can know about safety, because the information is not yet available. Should the profession, or an individual social worker, opt to assume a role in the area of medications, there are many ethical issues that will require thorough discussion. If a social worker assumes responsibility, he/she can't later argue that "social workers weren't trained in this area, so it isn't our job." If a professional elects to adopt an area of responsibility, then it is incumbent upon him/her to become trained. Since sources of information are diffuse and often written in technical language, the task is daunting.

REFERENCES

Alliance Pharmaceutical Corp. Office of Research and Development: Pharmaceutical Manufacturers Association. Website, 2002.

Angel, M. (2000). Is academic medicine for sale? *New England Journal of Medicine, 342,* 1516-1518.

Appelbaum, P. S., Lidz, C. W., & Meisel, A. (1987). *Informed consent: Legal theory and clinical practice*. New York: Oxford University Press.

Babyak, M., Blumenthal, J. A., Herman, S., Khatri, P., Doraiswamy, M., Moore, K., Craighead, W. E., Baldewicz, T. T. & Krishnan, K. R. (2000). Exercise treatment for major depression: Maintenance of therapeutic benefit at 10 months. *Psychosomatic Medicine, 62,* 633-638.

Bech, P., Cialdella, P., Haugh, M. C., Birkett, M. A., Hours, A., Boissle, J. P., & Tollefson, G. D. (2001). Meta-analysis of randomised controlled trials of fluoxetine v. placebo and tricyclic antidepressants in the short-term treatment of major depression. *British Journal of Psychiatry, 176,* 421-428.

Brandes, L. J., Arron, R. J. Bogdanovic, R. P., Tong, J., Zaborniak, C. L. F., Hogg, G. R., Warrington, R. C., Fang, W., & LaBella, F. S. (1992). Stimulation of malignant growth in rodents by antidepressant drugs at clinically relevant doses. *Cancer Research, 52,* 3796-3800.

Breggin, P. R. (1994). *Talking back to Prozac*. New York: St. Martin's Press.

Brown, G. L., & Linnoila, M. I. (1990). CSF serotonin metabolite (5-HIAA) studies in depression, impulsivity, and violence. *Journal of Clinical Psychiatry, 51,* 31-41.

Bulik, C. M., Carpenter, L. L., Kupfer, D. J., & Frank, E. (1990). Features associated with suicide attempts in recurrent major depression. *Journal of Affective Disorders, 18,* 29-37.

Byrne, S., & Rothschild, A. J. (1998). Loss of antidepressant efficacy during maintenance therapy: Possible mechanisms and treatments. *Journal of Clinical Psychiatry, 59,* 279-288.

Cauchon, D. (2000). FDA advisers tied to industry. *USA Today,* September 25.

Code of Ethics of the National Association of Social Workers. (1996). National Association of Social Workers. Washington, DC.

Coryell, W., Scheftner, W., Keller, M., Endicott, J., Maser, J., & Klerman, G. L. (1993). The enduring psychosocial consequences of mania and depression. *American Journal of Psychiatry, 150,* 720-727.

Critser, G. (1996). Oh, how happy we will be. *Harper's magazine, 292,* 39-49.

Crowson & Marro (1995). Antidepressant therapy: A possible cause of atypical cutaneous lymphoid hyperplasia. *Archives of Dermatology, 131*, 925-929.

Elkin, I., Shea, T., Watkins, J. T., Imber, S. D., Sotsky, S. M., Collins, J. F., Glass, D. R., Pilkonis, P. A., Leber, W. R., Docherty, J. P., Fiester, S. J., & Parloff, M. B. (1989). National Institute of Mental Health treatment of depression collaborative research program. *Archives of General Psychiatry, 46*, 971-982.

Fava, G. A. (2002). Long-term treatment with antidepressant drugs: The spectacular achievements of propaganda. *Psychotherapy and Psychosomatics, 63*, 127-132.

Fava, G. A. (2001). Conflict of interest and special interest groups. *Psychotherapy and Psychosomatics, 70*, 1-5.

Fava, G. A. (1998). All our dreams are sold. *Psychotherapy and Psychosomatics, 67*, 191-193.

Fava, G. A. (1995). Holding on: Depression, sensitization by antidepressant drugs, and the prodigal experts. *Psychotherapy and Psychosomatics, 64*, 57-61.

Fava, G. A. (1994). Do antidepressants and antianxiety drugs increase chronicity in affective disorders? *Psychotherapy and Psychosomatics, 61*, 125-131.

File, S. E., Kenny, P. J., & Cheeta, S. (2000). The role of the dorsal hippocampal serotonergic and cholinergic systems in the modulation of anxiety. *Pharmacology, Biochemistry, and Behavior, 66*, 65-72.

Frank, E., Kupfer, D. J., & Perel, J. M. (1989). Early recurrence in unipolar depression. *Archives of General Psychiatry, 46*, 397-400.

Frank, E., & Thase, M. E. (1999). Natural history and preventative treatment of recurrent mood disorders. *Annual Review of Medicine, 50*, 453-468.

Garcia-Toro, M., Montes, J. M., & Talavera, J. A. (2001). Functional cerebral asymmetry in affective disorders: New facts contributed by transcranial magnetic stimulation. *Journal of Affective Disorders, 66*, 103-109.

George, M. S., Wassermann, E. M., Willaims, W. A., Steppel, J., Pascual-Leone, A., Basser, P., Hallett, M., & Post, R. M. (1996). Changes in mood and hormone levels after rapid-rate transcranial magnetic stimulation (rTMS) of the prefrontal cortex. *Journal of Neuropsychiatry and Clinical Neuroscience, 8*, 172-180.

Gilbody, S. M. & Song, F. (2000). Publication bias and the integrity of psychiatry research. *Psychological Medicine, 30*, 253-258.

Greenhouse, J. B., Stangl, D., Kupfer, K. J., & Prien, R. F. (1991). Methodological issues in maintenance therapy clinical trials. *Archives of General Psychiatry, 48*, 313-318.

Guze, S. B., & Robins, E. (1970). Suicide and primary affective disorder. *British Journal of Psychiatry, 117*, 437-448.

Handley, S. L. (1995). 5-hydroxytryptamine pathways in anxiety and its treatment. *Pharmacological Therapeutics, 66*, 103-148.

Hariri, A. R., Mattay, V. S., Tessitore, A., Kolachana, B., Fera, F., Goldman, D., Egan, M. F., & Weinberger, D. R. (2002). Serotonin transporter genetic variation and the response of the human amygdala. *Science, 297*, 400-403.

Hervas, I., Vilaro, M. T., Romero, L., Scorza, M. C., Mengod, G., & Artigas, F. (2001). Desensitization of 5-HT (1A) autoreceptors by a low chronic fluoxetine dose effect of the concurrent administration of WAY-100635. *Neuropsychopharmacology, 24*, 11-20.

Hoehn-Saric, R., Lipsey, J. R., & McLeod, D. R. (1990). Apathy and indifference in patients on fluvoxamine and fluoxetine. *Journal of Clinical Psychopharmacology, 10*, 343-345.

Hollister, L. E. (1988). Antidepressants. In H. H. Goldman (Ed.), *Review of general psychiatry* (pp. 529-599). San Mateo, CA: Appleton & Lange.

Hollon, S. D. (1996). The efficacy and effectiveness of psychotherapy relative to medications. *American Psychologist, 51*, 1025-1030.

Hollon, S. D., DeRubeis, R. J., Shelton, R. C., & Weiss, B. (2002). The emperor's new drugs: Effect size and moderation effects. *Prevention & Treatment*, Volume 5, Article 28. Available on World Wide Web: http://www.journals.apa.org/prevention.

Jacobs, B. L., & Fornal, C. A. (1999). Activity of serotonergic neurons in behaving animals. *Neuropsychopharmacology, 21*, 9S-15S.

Kahn, A., Kahn, S. R., Leventhal, R. M., & Brown, W. A. (2001). Symptom reduction and suicide risk in patients treated with placebo in antidepressant clinical trials: A replication of the Food and Drug Administration Database. *International Journal of Neuropsychopharmacology, 4*, 113-118.

Keller, M. B., Kocsis, J. H., Thase, M. E., Gelenberg, A. J., Rush, A. J., Koran, L., Schatzberg, A., Russel, J., Hirschfeld, R., Klein, D., McCullough, J. P., Fawcett, J. A., Kornstein, S., LaVange, L., & Harrison, W. (1998). Maintenance phase efficacy of sertraline for chronic depression: A randomized controlled trial. *Journal of the American Medical Association, 280*, 1665-1672.

Keller, M. B., McCullough, J. P., Klein, D. N., Arnown, B., Dunner, D. L., Gelenberg, A. J., Markowitz, J. C., Nemeroff, C. B., Russell, J. M., Thase, M. E., Trivedi, M. H., & Zajecka, J. (2000). A comparison of nefazodone, the cognitive-behavioral analysis system of psychotherapy, and their combination for the treatment of chronic depression. *New England Journal of Medicine, 18*, 1462-1470.

Kirsch, I., Moore, T. J., Scoboria, A., & Nicholls, S. A. (2002). The emperor's new drugs: An analysis of antidepressant medication data submitted to the U.S. Food and Drug Administration. *Prevention & Treatment, 5*, Article 23. Available on World Wide Web: http://www.journals.apa.org/prevention/volume1/pre0010002a.html.

Kirsch, I., & Sapirstein, G. (1998). Listening to Prozac but hearing placebo: A meta analysis of antidepressant medication. *Prevention & Treatment, 1*, Article 0002a. Available on the World Wide Web: http://www.journals.apa.org/prevention/volume1/pre001002a.html.

Kocsis, J. H., Frances, A. J., Voss, C., Mason, B. J., Mann, J. J., & Sweeney, J. (1988). Imipramine and social-vocational adjustment in chronic depression. *American Journal of Psychiatry, 145*, 997-999.

Lidz, C. W., Meisel, A., Zerubavel, R., Carter, M., Sestak, R. M., & Roth, L. (1984). *Informed consent*. New York: Guilford Press.

Linnoila, M., De Jong, J., & Virkkunen, M. (1989). Family history of alcoholism in violent offenders and impulsive fire setters. *Archives of General Psychiatry, 46*, 613-616.

Littrell, J. (1994). Relationship between time since reuptake-blocker antidepressant discontinuation and relapse. *Experimental and Clinical Psychopharmacology, 2*, 82-94.

Littrell, J. (1995). Clinical practice guidelines for depression in primary care: What social workers need to know. *Research on Social Work Practice, 5,* 131-151.

Littrell, J., & Ashford, J. B. (1995). Is it proper for psychologists to discuss medications with clients? *Professional Psychology: Research and Practice, 26,* 238-244.

MacKay, F. J., Dunn, N. R., & Mann, R. D. (1999). Antidepressants and the serotonin syndrome in general practice. *British Journal of General Practice, 49,* 871-874.

Maier, S. F., & Watkins, L. R. (1998). Stressor controllability, anxiety, and serotonin. *Cognitive Therapy and Research, 22,* 595-613.

Mann, J. J. (1999). Role of the serotonergic system in the pathogenesis of major depression and suicidal behavior. *Neuropsychopharmacology, 21,* 99S-105S.

Mårtensson, B., Nyberg, S. Toresson, G., Brodin, E., & Bertilsson, L. (1989). Fluoxetine treatment of depression. Clinical effects, drug concentrations, and monoamine metabolites and N-terminally extended substance P in cerebrospinal fluid. *Acta Psychiatrica Scandanavia, 79,* 586-596.

Mason, P. J., Morris, V. A., & Balcezak, T. J. (2000). Serotonin syndrome: Presentation of 2 cases and review of the literature. *Medicine, 79,* 201-209.

Miller, I. W., Keitner, G. I., Schatzberg, A. F., Klein, D. N., Thase, M. E., Rush, A. J., Markowitz, J. C., Schlager, D. S., Kornstein, S. G., Davis, S. M., Harrison, W. M., & Keller, M. B. (1998). The treatment of chronic depression, III: Psychosocial functioning before and after treatment with sertraline or imipramine. *Journal of Clinical Psychiatry, 59,* 608-619.

Mintz, J., Mintz, L. I., Arruda, M. J., & Hwang, S. S. (1992). Treatments of depression and the functional capacity to work. *Archives of General Psychiatry, 49,* 761-768.

Mirrow, S. (1991). Cognitive dysfunction associated with fluoxetine. *American Journal of Psychiatry, 148,* 948-949.

Nemeroff, C. B. (2001). Progress in the battle with the black dog: Advances in the treatment of depression. *American Journal of Psychiatry, 158,* 1555-1557.

Opbroek, A., Delgado, P. L., Laukes, C., McGahuey, C., Katsanis, J., Moreno, F. A., & Manber, R. (2002). Emotional blunting associated with SSRI-induced sexual dysfunction. Do SSRIs inhibit emotional responses? *International Journal of Neuropsychopharmacology, 5,* 147-151.

Paykel, E. S., Ramana, R., Cooper, Z., Hayhurst, H., Kerr, J., & Barocka, A. (1995). Residual symptoms after partial remission: An important outcome in depression. *Psychological Medicine, 25,* 1171-1180.

Pelligrino, T. C., & Bayer, B. M. (2002). Role of central 5-HT$_2$ receptors in fluoxetine-induced decreases in T lymphocyte activity. *Brain, Behavior, and Immunity, 16,* 87-103.

Posternak, M. A., & Miller, I. (2001). Untreated short-term course of major depression: A meta-analysis of outcomes from studies using wait-list control groups. *Journal of Affective Disorders, 66,* 139-146.

Preskorn, S. H., & Magnus, R. D. (1994). Inhibition of hepatic P-450 isoenzymes by serotonin selective reuptake inhibitors: In vitro and in vivo findings and their implications for patient care. *Psychopharmacology Bulletin, 30,* 251-259.

Quitkin, F. F., & Stewart, J. (1993). Loss of drug effects during continuation therapy. *American Journal of Psychiatry, 150,* 562-565.

Reed, S. M., & Glick, J. W. (1991). Fluoxetine and reactivation of the herpes simplex virus. *American Journal of Psychiatry, 148,* 949-950.

Rihmer, Z., Barsi, J., Arato, M., & Demeter, E. (1990). Suicide in subtypes of primary major depression. *Journal of Affective Disorders, 18,* 221-225.

Scott, J. (2000). Treatment of chronic depression. *New England Journal of Medicine, 342,* 1518-1520.

Stahl, S. M. (1998). Mechanism of action of serotonin selective reuptake inhibitors. *Journal of Affective Disorders, 51,* 215-235.

Sternbach, H. (1991). The serotonin syndrome. *American Journal of Psychiatry, 148,* 705-713.

Thase, M. E., Blomgren, S. L., Birkett, M. A., Apter, J. T., & Tepner, R. G. (1997). Fluoxetine treatment of patients with major depressive disorder who failed initial treatment with sertraline. *Journal of Clinical Psychiatry, 58,* 16-21.

Thase, M. E., & Kupfer, D. J. (1996). Recent developments in the pharmacotherapy of mood disorders. *Journal of Consulting and Clinical Psychology, 64,* 646-659.

Thase, M. E., Rush, J., Howland, R. H., Kornstein, S. G., Kocsis, J. H., Gelenberg, A. J., Schatzberg, A. F., Koran, L. M., Keller, M. B., Russell, J. M., Hirschfeld, R. M. A., LaVange, L. M., Klein, D. N., Fawcett, J., & Harrison, W. (2002). Double-blind switch study of imipramine or sertraline treatment of anti-depressant-resistant chronic depression. *Archives of General Psychiatry, 59,* 233-239.

Thomas, R. (1990). Fluvoxamine maleate: A review of its properties and therapeutic efficacy. In B. Leonard & P. Spencer (Eds.), *Antidepressants: Thirty years on* (pp. 354-371). London: Clinical Neuroscience Publishers.

Torrey, E. F. (2002). The going rate on shrinks: Big Pharma and the buying of psychiatry. *American Prospect, July 15,* 15-16.

Wilkes, M. S., Doblin, B. H., & Shapiro, M. F. (1992). Pharmaceutical advertisements in leading medical journals: Experts' assessments. *Annals of Internal Medicine, 116,* 912-919.

Complementary Practices
and Herbal Healing:
A New Frontier in Counseling Practice

Sophia F. Dziegielewski

SUMMARY. As a means of achieving increased levels of health and wellness, complementary methods such as alternative approaches and medicinal preparations are being utilized to supplement or replace what has been viewed as traditional health care practice. To promote effective, efficient, and comprehensive helping relationships, social workers need to be cognizant that clients are using these methods and products, and how this use can affect the health care services they receive. This article identifies and discusses some of the basic types of alternative practices, herbal preparations, essential oils, and flower essences; as well as, the problems that can result from inadequate knowledge of the use or misuse of these products. In conclusion, emphasis is placed on increasing social work awareness and education in this area. *[Article copies available for a fee from The Haworth Document Delivery Service: 1-800-HAWORTH. E-mail address: <docdelivery@haworthpress.com> Website: <http://www.HaworthPress.com> © 2003 by The Haworth Press, Inc. All rights reserved.]*

The original version of this paper was initially presented at the First National Internet Conference on Social Work and Psychopharmacology, February 3-24, 2003, sponsored by the Ittleson Foundation and the Virginia Commonwealth University School of Social Work in association with Psy Broadcasting Company.

[Haworth co-indexing entry note]: "Complementary Practices and Herbal Healing: A New Frontier in Counseling Practice." Dziegielewski, Sophia F. Co-published simultaneously in *Social Work in Mental Health* (The Haworth Social Work Practice Press, an imprint of The Haworth Press, Inc.) Vol. 1, No. 4, 2003, pp. 123-139; and: *Psychiatric Medication Issues for Social Workers, Counselors, and Psychologists* (ed: Kia J. Bentley) The Haworth Social Work Practice Press, an imprint of The Haworth Press, Inc., 2003, pp. 123-139. Single or multiple copies of this article are available for a fee from The Haworth Document Delivery Service [1-800-HAWORTH, 9:00 a.m. - 5:00 p.m. (EST). E-mail address: docdelivery@haworthpress.com].

Digital Object Identifier: 10.1300J200v01n04_08

KEYWORDS. Herbal preparations, alternative practice, counseling practice

In the counseling setting, many social workers support the pronounced movement toward helping clients to take charge of their own mental and physical health; thereby, encouraging time-limited interventions that promote and maintain health and wellness. Furthermore, the proliferation of products designed to improve well-being has subsequently influenced the unprecedented growth of this multibillion-dollar industry (Foster & Tyler, 2000). For many social workers, competent practice involves assisting clients that use complimentary and/or alternative practices, herbal preparations, and essential oils or fragrances to enhance and support individual well-being. This extensive use makes awareness and knowledge on the part of the social worker essential as many times these products and techniques are utilized within the intervention process.

THE EXPLOSION OF HEALTH AND WELLNESS EFFORTS

For many individuals there is a pronounced movement toward taking charge of their own mental and medical health, which encourages the use of alternatives or supplements to traditional medical care. Whether out of cultural preferences, or dissatisfaction with the increasingly impersonal treatment from health care providers, individuals are using complementary approaches such as acupuncture, massage, homeopathic remedies, herbs, essential oils, and flower essences and a host of other non-allopathic treatments. It is becoming increasingly important for social workers to have adequate knowledge of these alternatives, since many of them have the potential to either interfere or intensify the actions of traditional medications and treatments (Dziegielewski, 2002; Dziegielewski & Sherman, 2003).

COMPLEMENTARY APPROACHES

Medical treatments in this country remain varied and can range from home remedies shared among family and friends to medications prescribed by a physician. For the most part, there are three primary approaches to the delivery of health care: traditional mainstream medicine, alternative medicine and complementary or integrative medicine (Dziegielewski & Sherman, 2003). In this country, the most traditional and widely used form of mainstream medicine involves standard drug therapies and surgical interventions. For the most part, traditional medical practitioners do not understand or condone the use of alternative therapies. If a client fears a physician may be opposed to non-traditional methods of treatment, he or she may not mention using it. In other cases, clients may simply avoid traditional medical approaches because of the invasiveness that can result. For example, in heart disease a client may decide that rather than having an operation to correct the problem an alternative treatment consisting of a low fat vegetarian diet, stress management, moderate exercise and group counseling is more desirable (McCall, 1998). For some clients, alternative approaches to traditional medical care can provide reasonable alternatives (Barrett, 1998). Regardless, of whether social workers support the use of non-traditional or holistic methods, they should always recommend that clients use the interventions proven to work. For example, in childhood leukemia conventional therapies can yield an 80% cure rate; therefore, it would seem unreasonable to switch to something that does not have as reasonable a chance of success (Stehlin, 1995).

A second approach to medical care that has recently gained in popularity is *alternative medicine*. According to Stehlin (1995), most alternative approaches consist of any medical practice or intervention utilized instead of conventional treatment. Unfortunately, many times these practices lack sufficient documentation on safety and efficacy. These varied approaches often involve techniques such as touch therapy and massage (e.g., acupressure), chiropractic, magnets, herbals and naturopathic remedies. Further techniques that allow for mind and body control, such as herbal preparations and spiritual healing, are also used. See Table 1 for a summary and quick reference for some of the different alternative approaches. When clients express interest in this type of therapy, it is important for social workers to encourage their clients to utilize the services of alternative practitioners that are licensed and/or certified.

Today in practice, it is possible to use a complementary or integrative approach (Gottelieb, 1995). The complementary or integrative perspective combines traditional approaches to therapy such as prescription medications, and augments or supplements this intervention regime with alternative approaches. Knowledge of this combined approach is essential because in 1997 alone, 42 percent of Americans used some type of alternative therapy, spending over $27 billion (Eisenberg, Da-

TABLE 1. Some Alternative Therapies

Alternative Medicine Systems

Traditional Chinese Medicine (TCM)–uses herbs, acupuncture, acupressure (shiatsu, tsabu, jin shin, jujitsu), and physical exercise like t'ai chi chian or qigong

Ayurveda–uses pranayama (alternate nostril breathing), abhyanga (rubbing skin with oil, usually sesame), rasayana (herbs and mantras during meditation), yoga, panchakarma (intense cleansing therapy including diaphoretics, diuretics, cathartics, and emetics), and herbal remedies

Naturopathy–holistic approach using homeopathy, vitamin and mineral supplements, physiotherapy, TCM, stress management, and herbs

Homeopathy–uses homeopathic (minute doses of herb, mineral or animal products) remedies as catalysts to aid body's inherent healing mechanism. Correct remedy treats the physical, emotional, and mental symptoms

Osteopathy–uses diagnostic and treatment techniques similar to medical practitioners, but also treats the musculo-skeletal system with adjustive maneuvers

Chiropractic–diagnoses and treats illnesses that affect the nerves, muscles, bones and joints by relieving pressure through manipulation

Environmental Medicine–focuses on the effect of chemicals, such as pesticides, food preservatives, car exhaust fumes, and formaldehyde, on the immune system. Uses nutritional supplements, immuno-therapy, and desensitization

Mind/Body Therapies

Hypnotherapy–technique of focused attention; especially helpful for pain management, addictions, and phobias

Biofeedback–relaxation technique to enable people to gain control over autonomic responses, such as heart rate, blood pressure, and voluntary muscle contractions

Relaxation Techniques–autogenic training, progressive muscle relaxation, meditation

Bodywork

Massage–lymphatic massage, neuromuscular (deep tissue) massage, rolfing (fascia manipulation)

Postural/Energy Therapies–focuses on relationship between the musculo-skeletal system and body movement. Alexander Technique (corrects muscle and joint coordination, balance and ease of movement), Feldenkreis (improves coordination and increases awareness of bodily functions involved with movement), and Therapeutic Touch

Dietary Supplements

Nutritional Supplements–deficiencies are determined through blood, stool, urine and hair analyses. Adverse reactions between medications and supplements can occur

Orthomolecular Medicine–uses mega doses of supplements; found useful for hyper-cholesterolemia and AIDS

Botanical Medicine–herbs are prescribed for specific symptoms

(Information obtained from Integrative Medicine Communications, 1998)

vid, Ettner et al., 1998). Furthermore, so much interest has been generated in alternative therapies that in 1992 the National Institutes of Health established the Office of Alternative Medicine (OAM) with a budget of $2 million. This trend has continued, and in the year 2000 the National Center for Complementary and Alternative Medicine (NCCAM), established by Congress as a replacement for OAM, had a budget of $68.7 million.

In addition, more than 60 percent of physicians from a wide range of specialties recommended alternative therapies to their clients or for themselves at least once (Borken, Neher, Anson, & Smoker, 1994). Utilizing an integrated approach, health care practitioners often recommend folic acid to prevent birth defects, Vitamin E to promote a healthy heart, or Vitamin C to boost the client's immune system. This movement toward alternative practices is becoming so prominent that many United States medical schools are now offering elective courses in complementary/alternative medicine (Wetzel, Eisenberg, & Kaptchuk, 1998). Unfortunately, education in this area is still in need of progress as evidenced by a recent University of Mississippi study in which 60 percent of retail pharmacists stated that they learned about herbal medicines from their own patients (Kroll, 1997).

THE USE OF HERBAL PREPARATIONS

This blossoming market has clearly attracted national attention and America, like so many other countries, has joined what appears to make alternative or herbal strategies the medicine of choice for over 70% of our world's population (Goeddeke-Merickel, 1998a; 1998b; 1998c). Plants and herbs in particular have constituted an ancient form of medicine that has been in existence for thousands of years. These medications are particularly popular in countries within Asia and Europe, particularly Germany, France, and Italy.

For the most part, herbal medicines are derived from plants, leaves, roots and flowers. There are numerous ways that these substances can be prepared and used. The most common usage is in the form of an *extract*, which can be in liquid, powdered or of a viscous nature. Often times the concentrations are derived from plant parts that have been either *macerated* (softening a solid by soaking it in a liquid) or *percolated* (a liquid containing the solid portion separated from the plant matter). Herbal remedies are often processed as *volatile oils*, in which the concentrates of active plant parts are left as the result of a distillation process. Another type of herbal remedies is the *tincture*, in which alcohol and hydroalcohol solutions are derived from the botanicals resulting in low concentrations of the active ingredients. When an extract is labeled *standardized*, a process has been implemented in which the unwanted components are removed and the more concentrated active ingredients remain.

Herbal preparations that are prepared as *teas* remain very popular. Teas consist of any herb that is capable of *infusion*. The term infusion means to boil the herb and later steep and strain it for use. Using hot water is probably the most common type of infusion and results from boiling the water and adding it to a cup of tea. A second way to prepare teas is called *decoction*. In this method, the tea mixture is prepared by adding it to cold water and later covered, boiled, simmered and strained for optimum use. In the cold maceration process the tea is mixed with tap water, covered and left to stand for six to eight hours, and when completed the mixture is strained and ready for use. There are many types of herbal preparations and a brief list is provided in Table 2 that highlights what are often considered the reasons for general use.

To date, there are well over 600 medicinal herbs available to the consumer (PDR for Herbal Medications, 1999) with little government oversight or regulation and little standardized testing to clearly establish their effectiveness (Foster & Tyler, 2000). Since herbal medications have received an upsurge of interest in the 1990s, they have clearly gotten the attention of the FDA. One of the greatest concerns for all social workers in accepting and supporting clients who utilize these types of preparations is the assumption that because herbals are natural–they must be safe (Dziegielewski, 2002; Rosch, 2000; Vazquez & Aguera-Ortiz, 2002). Unfortunately, nothing could be further from the truth. What is most startling is that considering their long history and traditions as medicinal remedies, little formal research has been completed that quantifies the effectiveness of their use.

It is also assumed that there is little relationship between prescription medications and those that are herbal based; yet, many prescription medications are created similarly. For example, most professionals do not realize that approximately 25% of all the pharmaceutical drugs used today are derived from herbs (Gruenwald, 1999). This means that many of the drugs used today adapt and freely utilize these ingredients in their composition. Aspirin, for example, a commonly used pain reliever, is derived from the bark of the White Willow tree; and, Taxol, a medication used in cancer treatment, comes directly from the Pacific Yew tree. Another example is the problems and interaction effects that can result

TABLE 2. Herbal Preparations

Herbal Preparation	Description	Other Names	Indications Usages	Precautions	Drug Interactions	Dosage/ Types
Cascara or Cascara Sagrada	Dried Bark	Yellow Bark Dogwood Bark	Constipation	Electrolyte imbalance Gastrointestinal Complaints Carcinogensis	Thiazide Diuretics Antiarrythmics	425 mg.-850mg Oral capsule or liquid
Capsicum (Cayenne)	Dried Ripe Fruit Flower	Cayenne Herbal Cayenne Pepper	Muscular Tensions Rheumatism	Hematologic Hyper-sensitivity Respiratory	Aspirin and Salicylic acid	400-500 mg External usage
Chaste Tree Berry	Dried Ripe Fruit	Chaste-berry Powder Vitex	Pre-menstrual Menopausal	Rashes	Dopamine–Receptor Antagonists	30-40 mg Oral, capsule, liquid
Dong Quai or Black Cohosh	Fresh and Dried Root	Remifemin	Premenstrual Syndrome (PMS)		anti-hypertensive medications	60 mg-545mg oral or external
Echinacea	Roots, Leaves or Whole plant parts	Echinacea Purpurea Black Sampson Purple Coneflower	Cold/Cough Fever Wounds	Nausea Hypersensitivity Rashes	Cyclosporine Corticosteriods	6 to 9 ml Oral or External Use
Evening Primrose	Oil from ripe seeds	Mega Prim-rose Oil	Neuro-derma titas Pre-menstrual Menopausal	Seizures in Pt's with Schizo-phrenia	Drugs related to those being treated to lower seizure threshold	500 mg Orally
Feverfew	Dried Leaves	Featherfew Feather foil	Migraine Arthritis Allergies	Gastro-intestinal Skin Muscular-skeletal	Thrombolytics Anticoagulants Platelet aggregation	200-250 mg for Migraine oral
Garlic	Fresh Dried Bulb	Garlicin Poor Man's Treacle	Arterio-sclerosis Hyper-tension Cholesterol Levels	Allergic Reactions Gastro-intestinal Hematological	Anticoagulants Aspirin	4 gm fresh daily or 8 mg oil form
Ginger	Fresh Dried Root (Rhizome)	Ginger Root Ginger Kid	Appetite Motion Sickness Dyspeptic	Hyper-sensitivity dermatitis	Anticoagulants Antithrom-bolytic agents	100mg-1000mg oral, tea, powder
Ginkgo	Dried Leaves	Ginkgo Biloba Ginkgold Quanterra	Short-term Memory Concent-ration Vertigo	Blood Pressure Fertility Hematological Effects	Anti-throm-bolytic agents Inhibitory effect on platelet-activating factor	40 mg to 80 mg three times daily oral

TABLE 2 (continued)

Herbal Preparation	Description	Other Names	Indications Usages	Precautions	Drug Interactions	Dosage/ Types
Ginseng	Fresh Dried Root	Ginsana Chinese Red Panax Siberian	Lack of Stamina Fatigue Stress	Cardiovascular Diabetes Hypertension Breast Nodularity Vaginal Bleeding	Insulin Hypo-glycemic effects Warfarin Antiplatelet agents, MAOI	1-2gm root tea, powder, tablet
Goldenseal	Dried Root (Rhizome)	Hydrastis canadensis	Irregular Menstruation Bronchitis Herpes	Pregnancy Digestive disorders	Berberine Heparin Decreased B Absorption	250 mg- 500 mg oral
Gotu Kola	Dried above ground plant parts	Centella Asiatica Indian Pennywort	Memory "Brain Food" Skin diseases Depression	Allergic contact dermatitis	*Does not contain Caffeine	400 mg- 500 m oral
Grape or Grape seed	Leaves and Seeds	Vitis Vinifera Activin	Headache Skin diseases	Inhibition Intestinal enzyme activity		150mg- 600mg oral
Green Tea	Dried Fresh Leaves	Chinese Tea Green tea extract	Cancer Hyper- tension Dental Caries	Gastric Irritation Cardiovascular Pregnancy and Children	Reabsorption of alkaline medications	300 mg- 400 mg pill or tea form
Guarana or Guarana seed	Dried crushed seed paste	Paullinia Cupana	Headache Cerebral stimulant	Cardiac disorders Panic and anxiety disorders	Diuretic action of Guarana may lead to hypokalemia	800 to 1000 mg oral
Kava Kava	Dried root (Rhizome)	Piper Methy- sticum Ava Pepper	Nervousness Insomnia Gastritis	Central Nervous System: Dyskinesia Weight loss	Alcohol Alprazolam CNS depressants Dopamine	150 mg- 300 mg twice a day, oral
Saw Palmetto	Dried Ripe Fruit	Serenoa Repens Sabal	Prostate Complaints Irritable Bladder	Anti-estrogenic effects Hormonal effects	Hormonal drugs Pregnancy	1-2 gm or 320mg extract
St. Johns Wort	Fresh flowers, dried above ground plant parts	Hypericum Perforatum Amber Goatweed	Anxiety Depression Skin inflammation Blunt injuries Wounds Burns	Restlessness Fertility effects Gastrointestinal Photo- sensitivity	MAOI's and SSRI's May inhibit iron absorption Cyclosporine Indinavir Ethinyloestradiol	500 to 900 mg/day for the depressed oral, tea, external topical

Table taken from Dziegielewski (2002). Information and abbreviated descriptions taken from the PDR for Herbal Medicines (2000), PDR for Prescription Medications (2000) and Dziegielewski & Leon (2001). Only some of the most common uses and dosage ranges for these substances are listed. Be advised that guidelines for dosing and the actual purpose of the herbal preparation vary tremendously based on source and variation, as well as how and why an herbal preparation is being taken.

from drinking grapefruit juice. One such case is what occurs to individuals who receive dialysis treatments, whereas the drinking grapefruit juice can prohibit the absorption of medications used in dialysis (Goeddeke-Merickel, 1998a). In addition, grapefruit juice can reportedly block the effects of medications used to treat cancer, hypertension, heart disease, and allergies (Mitchell, 1999; Rosch, 2000).

For so many clients, the belief that plant and tree products and juices are safe because these by-products are natural can create a false sense of security. The implications of this "natural is safe" mentality truly require further exploration and study as clients may be unaware that they are taking preparations that may create problems when combined with prescription or non-prescription drugs.

Mixing herbal remedies and prescription medicine does not always have to have a negative outcome. For some mixtures, the combination could be positive as the herbal remedies may compliment the other medications taken. Obviously, taking herbal preparations can enhance the quality of life for many. In addition, these complimentary preparations can supplement medication effects as well as augment and enhance the positive qualities of a medication. Regardless of whether there are positive or negative effects when dealing with any type of medication (herbal and natural included), it is essential for social workers to remind the client that every remedy that is strong enough to create an action can also cause a reaction (Dziegielewski, 2002).

For the FDA, probably the single largest concern is that these preparations lack formal regulation. Although regulation in some cases may be restrictive, when herbal products lack adequate controls and exist in a non-regulated environment, toxic reactions are more likely to occur (LaPuma, 1999). In the United States, the Dietary Supplement Health and Education Act (DSHEA) of 1994 allows herbs to be sold legally so long as they make no claims on the label for disease treatment (Kroll, 1997). This allows a loophole for popular products, primarily used for a specific purpose (i.e., St. John's Wort to address depression), to state on the label ambiguous terms for product use such as "promotes mental well-being" or "to improve mental health." To avoid legal penalties it is common for these herbal and natural product manufacturers to use vague terminology such as "to support body function" or "safely balances emotions"; and, as dietary supplements they are shielded from government oversight.

In terms of testing many professionals express concern over the lack of standardized and uniformed testing on herbal preparations. For the researcher, even if standardization is reached in a preparation trial there is no guarantee the same fresh or active ingredients will be present when the product is sold on the market to the consumer. Furthermore, with the lack of properly controlled studies, how do you really know who is taking the medicine; how much they are taking; and, whether they actually had the problem the herbal remedy was prepared for? With limited testing and methodological flaws, many of the herbal products cannot clearly link safety to efficacy nor can accurate testing occur of the claims the product is purported to address. One thing remains clear, in the United States more controlled studies in this area are needed (Bender, 1996; Rhodes-Kropf, 2001).

ESSENTIAL OILS

For thousands of years these essential oils have been used to enhance the environment and improve psychological and physiological well-being (Stevensen, 1996). Enjoying aromas or scents can vary from burning a scented candle, rubbing oils on the skin to enhance mood, to simply walking in a rose garden after a refreshing rain. Early reports of the power of essential oils in healing date back to Maurice-Rene Cattefosse, who accidentally discovered the healing benefits of these oils when he treated a third degree burn with lavender oil and experienced immediate relief. He continued the treatment for several weeks and healed without the expected scarring (Maxwell-Hudson, 1994). This documented experience was influential in the development of a branch of herbal medicine known as aromatherapy, in which these essential oils vaporize when heated, and the resulting plant aromas are used individually or in combination.

For the most part, essential oils are extracted from plants and herbs to treat conditions ranging from infections and skin disorders to immune deficiencies and stress. Through a process of steam distillation, essential oils are extracted from plant flowers, leaves, branches, or roots. The concentrated essence of aromatic plants is then used alone or in combination through inhalation, topical application or ingestion. These oils can be expensive but some are very concentrated requiring only a few drops to achieve the desired therapeutic effect. For the most part, these oils work by stimulating the olfactory system (the sense of smell), which connects to the emotional area of the brain in the areas of memory, breathing, and circulation (*A World of Aromatherapy*, 2001).

Massage as a method of application for essential oils allows the oil to penetrate the skin and underlying tissues. Different oils vary in their absorption rates and reach peak effectiveness at varying times following treatment. People with sensitive skin or allergies should be cautious about the use of essential oils. Some desired effects are mood enhancement with calming and sedative properties, as well as digestive, diuretic, decongestant, and pain relief. While these products are considered natural, they can be powerful and should not be used during pregnancy or with certain chronic health problems without the approval of a health care professional. For example, it has been advised that lavender with its calming effect and sedative properties should not be used during early pregnancy or in cases of low blood pressure (*A World of Aromatherapy*, 2001).

Essential oils are not the same as perfume or fragrance oils. Essential oils are derived from the true plants, whereas, perfume oils are artificially created fragrances and may not offer the same therapeutic benefits. Since essential oils are very potent, undiluted oil should never be applied directly to the skin as it may be toxic or burn the skin. For this reason all essential oils, prior to use on the skin, need to be diluted with carrier oil (sweet almond oil, apricot kernel oil, grape seed oil). When inhaled, it is important to remember that therapeutic benefit occurs when the oil molecules enter the lungs and are absorbed into the bloodstream. For the individual with sensitivities or allergies to a particular substance, an immediate reaction such as sneezing may result.

For the most part, essential oils are usually sold in very small dark bottles that vary greatly in quality and price. Various factors that can affect the quality and price of the oil include: the rarity of the plant; the country and conditions where the plant was grown; the quality standards of the distiller, and how much oil the plant produces. Essential oils can be purchased as a blended product. The advantage of the blend is the cost-savings from not having to buy each essential oil individually. The disadvantage is that the consumer has no control over the blend because the individual does not directly mix it (Aroma Web, 2001). See Table 3 for a sampling of oils and some potential uses.

The use of essential oils requires attention to the desired effects and the health of the recipient. Aromatherapy and the use of essential oils has been used by some practitioners for bacterial and viral infections, skin disorders, immune deficiencies, muscular disorders, arthritis, and cold sores. Today, with ongoing education and prudent and responsible use, aromatherapy remains an option as part of the varied spectrum of alternative therapies (Healthwell, 2001). Aromatherapy is considered an alternative intervention method for many conditions that were once remanded to prescription drugs.

TABLE 3. Essential Oils, Names and Comments

Common Name	Latin Name	Comments
Cedarwood	Cedrus atlantica	Yellow-orange oil with a mild woody scent. Powerful antiseptic.
Chamomile	Anthemis nobilis	Fresh, sweet herbaceous aroma. Relaxing and soothing oil.
Cypress	Cupressus sempervirens	Pale yellow-green oil with a smoky, sweet, balsamic aroma. Very astringent. Soothing and refreshing.
Eucalyptus	Eucalyptus citriodora	Has a penetrating camphoraceous woody-sweet scent. Stimulating oil. Antiseptic and anti-viral.
Fennel	Foeniculum vulgare	A clear essential oil with a deep, sweet, aniseed-like aroma. Good for digestion.
Frankincense	Boswellia thurfera/carterii	Also known as Olibanum. The oil has a rich, tenacious aroma. Comforting. Used for relaxation.
Geranium	Pelagonium graveolens	Pale yellow-green oil with a delicate, sweet, rose-like aroma. Appetite stimulant.
Ginger	Zingiber officinale	Has a rich gingery, warm, woody scent, preventative for stomach upset and seasickness.
Jasmine	Jasminum officinale	Dark orange-brown oil with an enticing sweet, warm, floral aroma. Anti-depressant and aphrodisiac.
Juniper	Juniperus communis	Distilled from juniper berries. Refreshing and invigorating oil. Antiseptic, astringent, and diuretic.
Lavender French	Lavendula augustifolium	A deep, soothing floral aroma. Analgesic, antiseptic, antidepressant, anti-bacterial, decongestant, and sedative.
Peppermint	Mentha piperita	Pale yellow color with a strong, penetrating grassy-mint aroma. Cooling and invigorating.
Rosewood	Aniba rosaeodora	Colorless oil with a sweet-woody, slightly spicy aroma.
Sandalwood	Santalum album	Pale yellow oil with a delightful smooth, tenacious, sweet-woody aroma. Sedative.
Tea Tree	Melaleuca alternifolia	Colorless oil with a fresh, spicy aroma similar to camphor. Anti-viral. Powerful stimulant to the immune system.
Thyme	Thymus serpyllum	Yellow-orange oil with a penetrating, herb-like, warm, spicy aroma. Antiseptic.

The above comprehensive and inclusive information and chart was adapted from: A Guide To Essential Oils And Their Uses Website at: http://www3.sympatico.ca/derekwatts/Oilcom.htm.

FLOWER ESSENCES

Recently, there has been a growing interest in using the scent of flowers to soothe the troubled spirit. Use of these substances has been related to addressing emotional problems as well as improving feelings of well-being. Some professionals contend that these methods can be quite advantageous as a supplement to brief psychotherapy by being less invasive with less potential for interaction than ingested herbal preparations. Utilizing flower essences requires that the blossoms of the plant be placed in water for several hours, allowing the sun to draw out the essence. The resulting solutions are then preserved with brandy and utilized in a diluted form. For example, a client might use a prescription medication in conjunction with Cassandra (a flower essence) to enhance a calming feeling. The use of flower essences can be a part of health care when a client wants natural treatment. When a client expresses interest in this type of treatment, the social worker should encourage the client to seek information about the desired remedy and methods of administration before trying it. A part of the health care education is to caution the client about potential allergic reactions and with known allergies; and serious investigation into the sources of flower essences should be conducted before incorporating this into the treatment regime. Furthermore, once therapy has begun, monitoring for adverse reactions should be a part of the evaluation of therapeutic effects.

In using flower therapies people usually find those traits (listed) that match a particular essence. For the most part, flower essences do not interfere with most medications, including homeopathic and herbal remedies; and, there are no known side effects, but as with any alternative therapy caution should always be exercised (Mendola, 1997a; 1997b). See Table 4 for sample of flower oils.

CONCLUSION AND FUTURE DIRECTIONS

In the counseling environment, it has become essential for social workers and other clinicians to become aware of the substances that clients are using and both the positive and negative results that can occur. According to Stehlin (1995), most alternative approaches lack safety and effectiveness information when used on certain diseases and conditions. Many health care providers and clients may not be aware of the effects these practices can have on the therapeutic environment. Practice reality reveals that the numbers of individuals using alternative

TABLE 4. Flower Essences for Emotional Situations

Flower Essences

Bleeding Heart: can be used to assist with moving beyond a relationship or to cope with the death of a loved one.

Chamomile: can be used to calm an individual.

Impatiens: can be used to calm an individual that is quick to get angry and is impulsive.

Morning Glory: can be used to wake an individual up in the morning without the use of stimulants.

Shasta Daisy: can be used to assist an individual to think more clearly.

Zinnia: can be used to lift mood.

Elm: can be used for everyday stress or feelings of being overwhelmed by responsibility.

Hornbeam: can be used for fatigued individuals who are under chronic stress.

Mimulus: can be used to help address anxiety.

Star of Bethlehem: can be used to help an individual relax.

White chestnut: can be used for everyday stress and can help bring about relaxed states making an individual more susceptible to sleep.

Wild Oat: can be used for stress.

*Information adapted from the work of Flower Essence Repertory by Patricia Kaminski and Richard Katz, pamphlet published by the Flower Essence Society. The following "Flowers for Stress" are taken from Heathwell.com (Mendola, 1997a;1997b). These flowers are specifically related to use for stressed individuals and for stressful situations. Always remember these are suggested uses and the effects on the individual can vary tremendously.

therapies is rising, and clients utilizing integrated approaches may not tell the health care provider what strategies are being used (Cary, 1998; Dziegielewski & Leon, 2001). Poor or the general lack of communication can make it very difficult for health care practitioners to assess the needs of the client. Furthermore, this total lack of supervised care can clearly complicate current treatment regimes. Not knowing what a client is taking can put the client at significant risk for problematic interactions and synergistic effects. In the brief therapeutic encounter, it is important to take the time to listen to what clients think, feel and say. The resulting rapport can help clients to feel more comfortable facilitating discussion of what is being taken and why.

For many social workers, informal learning about alternative medicines is a sign of the times, as many professionals, including pharmacists, lack formal professional training in the area of herbal remedies

(Kroll, 1997). This means that many times clients are expected to educate the professionals they are seeing regarding what herbal preparations they are taking and why. This is particularly difficult with the lack of controls and the conflicting, ambiguous information often found in this area. When health care professionals have trouble understanding these products, imagine how complicated it can be for the clients utilizing them.

For many clients, particularly those with chronic or terminal conditions, conventional therapies have indeed fallen short and psychotherapy can simply take too long (McCall, 1998). These individuals want to feel more in control of their health and want the convenience of a pill or a quick fix. When looking closely at the alternative or complimentary forms of medicine it is easy to see how they have gained interest. Conventional and unconventional approaches can be limited in terms of therapeutic effect and expense, and both types of treatments can yield potentially negative side effects or toxic outcomes if used inappropriately.

In the practice environment, there is a growing movement to integrate alternative and conventional health care as a means of increasing therapeutic speed and effectiveness. Clients need to be encouraged to share information about the substances they are taking. Combining herbs, oils, flower essences and other supplements with prescription drugs can augment practice–but it can also create unpleasant and even hazardous consequences. If all practitioners involved in helping a client to progress are not informed about what the client is taking, the professional will be unable to use his/her professional expertise to help the client determine if this is the best remedy available. For social workers, it is important to encourage clients to inform health care providers of all natural remedies taken. This information will allow the health care professional to become better prepared regarding the effects that these natural remedies can have on treatment outcomes. Social workers should also encourage client self-determination allowing the individual to make informed decisions in terms of what is best for them. Clients do not have to accept and automatically commit to a traditional approach to medical care (Seligson, 1998). By understanding that there may be a reluctance to discuss the use of natural remedies with the mainstream medical community, social workers can help clients to prepare for such discussions. Information provided can help clients decide what questions will facilitate the conversation with the physician or nurse practitioner.

In closing, effective, efficient, and comprehensive helping relationships require that social workers not ignore that a client is utilizing complimentary or alternative approaches. In addition, the social worker needs to help the client explore whether this form of treatment could potentially benefit or harm intervention progress. Alternative forms of intervention can also serve as a preventative measure helping to ensure client well-being. Social workers need to be aware of these techniques and remedies as providers of stress management strategies, relaxation techniques, and counseling. Keeping abreast of all forms of intervention is important to provide the best possible care for clients, while discouraging the use of medications and herbal preparations as being considered the only form of intervention when other therapeutic alternatives can prove to be supplemental or just as effective.

REFERENCES

A guide to essential oils and their uses: Essential oils, names, and comments. Retrieved October 21, 2001, from www.3.swsympatico.ca/derekwatts/Oilcom.htm

A World of Aromatherapy. Retrieved October 3, 2001 from the World Wide Web: *http://www.aworldofaromotherapy.com/aromotherapy-today.htm.*

Barrett, A. (1998). Hot war over herbal remedies. *Business Week, 33581,* 42.

Bender, K.J. (1996, October). St. John's Wort evaluated as an herbal antidepressant. *Psychiatric Times.* Retrieved July 6, 1999 from the World Wide Web: http://www.mhsource.com/edu/psytimes/p964058.html

Borken, J., Neher, J.O., Anson, O., & Smoker, B. (1994). Referrals for alternative therapies. *Journal of Family Practice, 39,* 6, 545-50.

Cary, C. (1998). St. John's Wort–The happy flower. *Times-News. http://www.timesnewsfreedom.com/news/stjohnwort.html*

Dziegielewski, S.F. (2002). Herbal Preparations and Social Work Practice. In A. Roberts and G. Green (Eds.), *Social Workers' Desk Reference.* New York: Oxford University Press.

Dziegielewski, S.F., & Leon, A. (2001). *Social Work Practice and Psychopharmacology.* New York: Springer Publishing.

Dziegielewski, S.F., & Sherman, P. (2003). Complementary Therapies: Tips and techniques for Health Care Social Workers. In S. Dziegielewski and Contributors, *Changing face of health care practice: Professional practice in managed behavioral health care* (Chapter 19). Springer: New York.

Eisenberg, D.M., David, R.B., Ettner, S.L., Appel, S., Wilkey, S., Van Rompay, M., & Kessler, R.C. (1998). Trends in alternative medicine use in the United States: Results of a follow-up national survey. *JAMA, 280,* 18, 1569-75.

Foster, S., & Tyler, V.E. (2000). *Tyler's honest herbal.* New York: The Haworth Herbal Press.

Goeddeke-Merickel, C.M. (1998a). Herbal medicine: Some dos and don'ts for dialysis patients. *For Patients Only.* March/April, 22-23.

Goeddeke-Merickel, C.M. (1998b). Alternative medicine and dialysis patients; Part II. *For Patients Only.* May/June, 19-20.

Goeddeke-Merickel, C.M. (1998c). Alternative medicine and dialysis patients: Part III. *For Patients Only.* July/August, 22 and 30.

Gottelieb, B. (1995). *New choices in natural healing.* Emmaus, PA: Rodale Press.

Gruenwald, J. (1999). *PDR for herbal medications.* Montvale, NJ: Medical Economics.

Healthwell. (n.d.). *Aromatherapy.* Retrieved October 21, 2001, from www.healthwell.com/healthnotes/Info/Aromatherapy.cfm?path=hw

Kroll, D.J. (1997). St John's Wort: An example of the problems with herbal medicine regulation in the United States. *Medical Sciences Bulletin,* September, 240, 1-5.

LaPuma, J. (1999). Danger of Asian patent medicines. *Alternative Medicine Alert: A Clinician's Guide to Alternative Therapies, 2,* 6, 71.

Maxwell-Hudson, C. (1994). *Aromatherapy Massage.* Boston: Houghton Mifflin.

McCall, M.D. (1998). *Alternative medicine: Is it for you?* Orlando Sentinel, May 12, 1998, Orlando, FL.

Mendola, K. (1997a, November). *Balance Emotions with Flower Essences.* Retrieved October 15, 2001 from Healthwell Web Site: http://www.healthwell.com/delicious-online/d_backs/Nov_97/hk.cfm

Mendola, K. (1997b, November). *Flowers For Stress.* Retrieved October 15, 2001 from Healthwell Web Site: *http://www.healthwell.com/delicious-online/D_backs/Nov_97/hk.cfm*

Mitchell, P. (1999). Grapefruit juice found to cause havoc with drug uptake. *Lancet, 353* (9161), 1335-1336.

Rhodes-Kropf, J. (2001, August). Achieving balance between herbal remedies and medical therapy on base rate [4 pages]. *Geriatrics* (on-line serial). Available: http://www.findarticles.com/cf_dls/m2578/8_56/78056239/print.jhtml

Rosch, P. (2000). Certain foods, drugs and supplements don't mix. *Health and Stress, X,* 11, 1-8.

Seligson, S.V. (1998). Melding medicines. *Health, May/June 1998,* 64-70.

Stehlin, I.B. (1995). An FDA guide to choosing medical treatments. *FDA Consumer, 29,* 10-14.

Stevensen, C.J. (1996). Aromatherapy. In M.S. Micozzi (Ed.), *Fundamentals of Complementary and Alternative Medicine* (pp. 137-148). New York: Churchill Livingstone.

Vazquez, I., & Aguera-Ortiz, L.F. (2002). Herbal products and serious side effects: A case of ginseng-induced manic episode. *ACTA Psychiatricia, 105,* 0001-690X, 76-78.

Wetzel, M.S., Eisenberg, D.M., Kaptchuk, T.J. (1998). Courses involving complementary and alternative medicine at U.S. medical schools. *JAMA, 280,* 9, 784-7.

Index

SPECIAL 25%-OFF DISCOUNT!

Order a copy of this book with this form or online at:
http://www.haworthpress.com/store/product.asp?sku=5126
Use Sale Code BOF25 in the online bookshop to receive 25% off!

Psychiatric Medication Issues
for Social Workers, Counselors, and Psychologists

____ in softbound at $14.96 (regularly $19.95) (ISBN: 0-7890-2401-2)
____ in hardbound at $29.96 (regularly $39.95) (ISBN: 0-7890-2400-4)

COST OF BOOKS _____
Outside USA/ Canada/
Mexico: Add 20%. _____

POSTAGE & HANDLING _____
US: $4.00 for first book & $1.50
for each additional book
Outside US: $5.00 for first book
& $2.00 for each additional book.

SUBTOTAL _____

In Canada: add 7% GST. _____

STATE TAX _____
CA, IL, IN, MIN, NY, OH, & SD residents
please add appropriate local sales tax.

FINAL TOTAL _____
If paying in Canadian funds, convert
using the current exchange rate,
UNESCO coupons welcome.

❏ **BILL ME LATER:**
Bill-me option is good on US/Canada/
Mexico orders only; not good to jobbers,
wholesalers, or subscription agencies.

❏ **Signature** _____

❏ **Payment Enclosed: $** _____

❏ **PLEASE CHARGE TO MY CREDIT CARD:**

❏ Visa ❏ MasterCard ❏ AmEx ❏ Discover
❏ Diner's Club ❏ Eurocard ❏ JCB

Account # _____

Exp Date _____

Signature _____
*(Prices in US dollars and subject to
change without notice.)*

PLEASE PRINT ALL INFORMATION OR ATTACH YOUR BUSINESS CARD

Name		
Address		
City	State/Province	Zip/Postal Code
Country		
Tel	Fax	
E-Mail		

May we use your e-mail address for confirmations and other types of information? ❏Yes ❏No
We appreciate receiving your e-mail address. Haworth would like to e-mail special discount
offers to you, as a preferred customer. **We will never share, rent, or exchange your e-mail
address.** We regard such actions as an invasion of your privacy.

Order From Your Local Bookstore or Directly From
The Haworth Press, Inc.
10 Alice Street, Binghamton, New York 13904-1580 • USA
Call Our toll-free number (1-800-429-6784) / Outside US/Canada: (607) 722-5857
Fax: 1-800-895-0582 / Outside US/Canada: (607) 771-0012
E-Mail your order to us: Orders@haworthpress.com

Please Photocopy this form for your personal use.
www.HaworthPress.com

BOF04